LOVE

In Search of a Reason for Living

Edited/authored by Paul Snyder – the editorial "we" is used to emphasize that most of materials and other content was assembled by and not original to, the author.

i

Contents

iv

What is This Book?

It is an essay about life, a book about you. Its purpose is to send you on a journey through your heart, mind, and soul. If you take the journey you will find in yourself the reason for living. If you care at all about life and people and yourself, you will take the journey.

If you are a humanist, a skeptic, or are just not sure what to believe, please read our entire book. We believe it represents an objective, rational, reasoned, search for a reason for living.

We begin our journey.

[If you have already read our book LifeNotes, you will notice that most of the text was taken directly from this book. There is a lot of duplication, however there are more chapters in this book and additional material in some of the chapters. This book has approximately double the content of LifeNotes, and further explains some of our conclusions. The repetition is for those who have not read LifeNotes and a restatement of our conclusions for those who have.]

Who Am I?

The day you were born you began a learning process that will continue for the rest of your life. You were, from the beginning, molded by your surroundings, parents, relatives, playmates, by all the general attitudes, ideas, and beliefs you came in contact with. As you grew older those early experiences affected, both consciously and subconsciously, what you felt and did about all the day to day things that went on around you. Each new year of life added to your past, changing the way you viewed every new day, influencing how you reacted to everything from the simplest daily routines to complex events touching you, your family, and the world you lived in.

You most likely met people from different backgrounds with differing ideas about life. If so you may have found yourself actively defending, modifying, or abandoning your early beliefs, adapting the various ideas you came in contact with to fit your developing perception of life. Perhaps new ideas were introduced to you by people with dynamic personalities who espoused one philosophy or another. Faced with the challenge of those ideas, you may have tenaciously defended your early beliefs, dismissing unfamiliar concepts with alarming ease. On the other hand, you may have completely abandoned your past and adopted new beliefs opposite to those you once cherished.

However, like most people, you probably belong to that vast river of humanity which seems to move along in a fairly discernible direction, concerned at any given minute with living that moment in the easiest, most pleasant way possible. If so, you were and are more or less able to blend ideas, feelings, philosophies, desires, and realities to justify what you want to do. Along with the majority of people, you were and are good at sending questions and ideas about the meaning of life and death, as well as thoughts and feelings about what is good and right, deep into the cloudy regions of your mind.

Whether we realize it or not, most of us are voluntary prisoners of our minds, unwilling to question who we are and what we believe, happy to simply roll along through life. Most of us will live from birth to death in a world we have fashioned from our past to suit our present. Many will find comfort through unquestioned acceptance of their family's, or friend's, religious or philosophical heritage. Few will stand free from their present beliefs and daily lives to ask what is life about? Who am I? What should I do? What will I do?

If there is meaning to life, and a reason for living, these questions must be answered. If there is a true meaning to life, nothing that you do, say, or think will change that truth. What good is it to live your life believing what you are doing is right if your beliefs are false and what you are doing is wrong? It is an understanding of life that we seek, a search for something in life worth living for.

You must be willing to recognize the answers when you find them. You cannot hide in the comfort of daily living. You must open your mind and accept whatever you discover, even if it does not fit what your life is and what you want it to be. If what we are saying is true, your willingness to understand is a willingness to grasp the very reason for your living. If the answers you find are different from those you have molded for yourself, you must decide whether to continue on the path you are on or go another way on a new path toward a new destination.

If You Are Who You Are Then Who Are You?

Each of us is born, we live lives of various lengths, and then we die. Each of us has, or perhaps develops, a separate nature and existence, a being, which is unique to us and sets us apart from every other person who lives or has ever lived. Indeed we share similar characteristics, but no two of us are the same person. You are you.

What makes each of us unique is the fact that we perpetually make choices between alternatives. Our choices seem to be far more than mechanical selections based on some complex biological decision making scheme. Rather, your choice seems to be based not only on what you believe will happen if you make a certain choice, but also on what you "want" to happen. You, as all of us do, possess the ability to engage in what we will call "rational thought", whereby each of us weighs many variables in a process that includes concepts of good and evil, right and wrong. "Rational thought", as we define it, is reasoned thought that presents us with choices between alternatives. You ultimately reach a point in your rational thinking where that certain quality of being which is unique to you takes over and you make your choice among the alternatives.

Biologists have demonstrated that the line between animal and human "thought" is not as clear as was once commonly assumed. There are animals that appear to have self-awareness, solve problems, communicate, exhibit emotions, etc. While there may be a very high degree of intelligence in the animal world, animals seem to lack the ability to make choices by consciously "thinking" about alternatives and consequences. It appears that only human beings possess the necessary consciousness and symbolic languages that allow us to engage in significant abstract thought.

For example, animals may or may not harm other animals, yet they do not appear to be able to make reasoned choices to harm or not to harm by considering whether it is right or wrong to do so. An animal may make a "choice" to act kindly toward another animal based in part on their "inherent personality" and "basic instincts". Yet it appears that an animal cannot make a rational, reasoned, choice to go against inherent personality and basic instincts. Human beings can choose to do that which they would not otherwise do, to go against what their instincts,

5

personality, and emotions tell them to do. We sometimes take this apparent distinction for granted. Rather than consider ourselves to be nothing more than highly evolved animals, we should recognize and give more consideration to our unique ability to engage in rational thought.

Unlike any animal, your choices are made after rational thought. Even though you have instinctive feelings for self-preservation, procreation, self-satisfaction, etc., decisions may be freely made for reasons and purposes totally opposite to those instincts. You can think about what you are going to do and can choose to do what you believe is right and good even if it places you in grave danger. Similarly, you can choose to do what you believe is wrong and evil even if you would instinctively do otherwise. Your decision is your decision, a product of your singular existence and being. Able to engage in rational thought, and to choose freely among various courses of action based on those thoughts, you are in a very real sense what you choose to be.

One of the oldest scientific controversies deals with what the significance of rational thought really is. Perhaps the most debated aspect of the question is whether or not rational thought actually gives us the ability to make "freewill" choices. Many scientists argue that every rational choice you make is in fact predetermined by your biochemical makeup. They admit that when you have a choice between two options you engage in both conscious and subconscious thought processes before making what you consider to be your decision. However they argue that no matter how convinced you are that your choice between A and B is your own, your brain chemistry actually dictates your selection. They suggest that your mind's decision-making processes cannot go beyond the level of chemical neurological activity. Therefore, even though your choices may in one sense still be said to be your own, they are in effect predetermined. Despite the agonizing doubts, careful thought, and numerous changes of mind that accompany daily decisions, many scientists believe the final decision would be totally predictable if they could decode your brain.

This idea of "determinism" manifests in the fatalism of some philosophies. Taken to its logical extreme, many scientists and philosophers believe in super-determinism, where all that is in the universe was in the past part of a closely related system in which "matter and energy" were joined. They view everything from sub-atomic particles to human beings as part of a universe whose destiny was forever set at creation by the forces between its constituent parts, and whose future unfolds in a billiard ball like progression of "predictable" actions. To this school of thought, humans are prisoners of subatomic laws that determine the behavior of atoms that determine the behavior of molecules that determine the behavior of nerve cells that determine the behavior of human brains that determine the behavior of human beings. Even though the chain is totally imperceptible to humankind, and a feeling of control exists as an inherent part of human existence, they insist that what seem to be "spontaneous" decisions and reactions are actually destined to occur without any possibility of variance.

While scientists are comfortable with the idea of an ordered and well-behaved universe, some view the complexity and reality of life as requiring events to be based on something less than absolute certainty. Some look to the uncertainty principle in quantum physics as a mechanism that would allow some degree of free choice. The problem is that those who champion the uncertainty principal can justifiably be called probability determinists, they argue for a determinism as certain as any, one that also sees humankind governed by forces beyond its control. The reality dictated by their brand of determinism is described by stating how likely it is that a particular event, chosen from a list of possible events, will occur. In other words, they can eliminate what cannot happen, can give you a list of events that might happen, and can even tell you how likely it is each individual item will take place, but they cannot tell you which of the possible events will in fact occur. From their viewpoint the exact future of the universe may be uncertain, yet it is still fundamentally predetermined.

Modern theories dealing with chaotic behavior tell us that because of the almost infinite number of possible combinations created by the interaction between objects we cannot complete the necessary calculations to determine what will in fact occur next. The popular example used to illustrate this is that if you want to precisely forecast the local weather you must calculate the number and exact location of all of the butterflies flapping their wings on the other side of the world. Furthermore, some mathematical problems may have no solutions, and seem to be fundamentally "non-computable". It is simply not known whether or not non-deterministic physical mechanisms exist in our universe.

Virtually all of the currently "favored" cosmologic theories dealing with chaos, complexity, and computability agree that given enough information and processing power (even if the required amounts

7

approach infinity) the probabilistic behavior of even the most complex system in our universe is "in theory" mathematically calculable. It is fair to say that all of the currently favored cosmologic theories conclude that our physical universe is, in some real sense, fully deterministic, while also concluding that it is beyond human ability to mathematically model our exact future.

In a universe that had no living organisms, determinism would not be as hard to accept as it is in our universe inhabited by living creatures. One can visualize a universe devoid of life where every rock, every speck of dust, every atom, every sub-atomic particle, follows a pattern which was forever fixed at creation, and which expands into the future with absolute precision. In an inanimate universe, it is not as difficult to accept that rocks, specks of dust, atomic particles, and even groups of these objects, have no "ability" to alter the course that the laws of physics dictate they follow.

It is much more difficult to accept that our universe, populated as it is by living organisms, is a totally deterministic one. If super-determinism is correct, we reach the intuitively unlikely result that the absolute time for every blink of our eyes is predetermined, and that every breath we take is taken at precise moments and in exact amounts! There is nothing we can do to alter any of our physical motions - even the slightest twitch of our body occurs at the very moment it was destined to occur by the forces acting in the first second of the universe. Every change of our minds is inevitable, every thought we have ever had was predetermined and occurred without any chance of alteration.

If we live in a fully deterministic world, I was destined before birth to write precisely the words contained in this paragraph on the day and at the time and on the computer I wrote them on, and when the universe was formed you were destined to read precisely the words contained in this paragraph on the day and at the time you are reading them. At the beginning of the world, not only were you predestined to be precisely where you are right now, but you were also destined to be wearing the clothes you are wearing, have every hair on your head the exact length that each one is, have every object in the room placed precisely where it is, etc. Every thought you are having about what I am saying was predetermined to occur without the slightest variation, even your in-stant reaction to this very sentence was set at creation. This simply does not "seem" to be what actually happens, we intuitively "feel" that we can make meaningful choices among alternatives, perhaps so, perhaps not.

Scientists and philosophers seem to accept determinism as being in control in the micro world of atoms, while detaching it from everyday macro life by also accepting the random nature of human choice. The problem is, where do we draw the line? If physical processes are fully causal, if A causes B that causes C, where do we find the freedom for A not to cause D? If the universe is not fully deterministic, could it be deterministic up to a point? Quantum theory may give us some wiggle room, as it allows every "hair on your head" to be a random length, but that length must be chosen between minimum and maximum allowed lengths. Perhaps the almost infinitely complex math behind the possible allowed combinations dilutes our fully deterministic processes, so that we may be said to at least be in partial control of our destiny, perhaps not.

This possibility leads many scientists and philosophers to assume that determinism is compatible with the existence of a physical, as opposed to a non-physical, consciousness that can be held to be morally responsible for its actions. They argue that no matter what happens at the cellular level, human beings make decisions using symbolic language and human intelligence. Yet it seems that to reach this conclusion the scientists and philosophers must ignore the fact that current physical theories are based on deterministic causal relationships, be they probabilistic or otherwise, and therefore lack any apparent mechanism for human freedom or responsibility.

They jump to the conclusion that because complex physical systems exhibit almost infinite complexity, the systems support some kind of metaphysical freedom. On closer examination this may not be justified, simply because in every accepted theory all observable physical systems, from Planck scale to the scale of the universe, appear at the very least to be governed by probabilistic determinism. The idea seems wrong that a physical consciousness based on purely deterministic physical processes might possess the freedom to make meaningful choices.

We note that no matter how predetermined your existence may be, it can be argued that "you" make freewill choices even if it is chemically determined what those choices will be, simply because "you" are the product of your biochemistry. While that argument, and variations of it, may be true by definition, it seems if we are to be held accountable

9

for our actions we should have a freedom of choice that can be anticipated to be found only in that which is beyond human chemistry.

Many scientists and philosophers argue that modern science has proven determinism to be "true". In fact, science has only begun to address the nature of human thought. On the sub-atomic level of quantum physics more questions have been raised than answers found. A few suggest that quantum uncertainty itself may provide a mechanism for choice through human ability to "manipulate" the probability of a given result. They suggest that human thought affects quantum processes in the components of brain neurons, resulting in non-deterministic outcomes. Others suggest that human thought exists in the "mind", something they theorize is separate from the physical "brain". Yet none of the current theories on conscious thought have been proven, they all remain speculative.

Even though current theories do not appear to allow for meaningful freewill, some scientists and philosophers argue that no matter how well ordered your chemical thought processes may be, you reach a point in each sequence of mental activity where the unique being which you are makes a decision. A decision that goes beyond the confines of conscious and subconscious biochemical processes. A choice made after considering the products of your biological thought processes along with abstract concepts of good and bad, right and wrong, etc. They believe the basic, profound aspect of human existence, which gives you the ability to engage in rational thought and makes you who you are, transforms your choices among alternatives into freewill decisions that transcend physical constraints.

It is difficult for those of us who have grown up in a scientific world to visualize, let alone accept, human thought extending beyond the chemical confines of the human mind. Yet there has been no scientific evidence (perhaps because no experiment has been devised that could test the hypothesis) that would refute the jump from predetermined biochemical thought to human thought controlled by individual beings. Because no one has explained the illusive quality that might make each human being unique and give them control over their decisions does not mean that it does not exist, nor does it mean it does exist.

Research into the nature of physical consciousness has demonstrated the incredible complexity, and fundamental mystery, of the human mind. Paradoxes associated with thought experiments suggest we have not yet begun to understand the basics of human consciousness and the

10

possibility of freewill. Even if the human mind can make meaningful statements about its most fundamental nature (it is not at all clear it can), nothing to date either proves or rules out the existence of human freewill. For the moment we ask you to accept the possibility that freewill exists beyond biological and physical constraints. We ask that you keep an open mind about the possible existence of individual control which makes your decisions truly your own.

Who Will You Be When You No Longer Are?

Warning! There is a risk that as you read our book you may think that we are suggesting that there is no "reason to live". That is not what we are saying at all! In fact we are saying the opposite, we have abundant hope that if you search your heart, mind, and soul, you will find in yourself the reason for living. If you are discouraged or depressed, please finish reading all of this book. Anyone who is, or becomes, seriously depressed should always seek immediate medical help. See Distress & Depression at the end of our book.

If in fact you do exercise meaningful freedom of choice, what good is it to be a unique human being if at your death you cease to exist? If you do not continue to exist in some form after death, what good are all the experiences, decisions, triumphs, defeats, all the moments of your life? If you do not survive the grave, if you return to the state of being that preceded your birth, then we suggest to you that nothing in fact does matter. While over the ages men and women have sought to perpetuate themselves through their children, their place in history, their role in society, and through intricate philosophical webs of existentialism and other essays on physical human being's importance, the fact of physical death remains. If each generation's death means the end of those individuals, then we are all faced with an endless cycle of creation and destruction, the meaning of which, if any, is beyond comprehension.

If there is anything in life we can count on occurring without fail it is physical death. The successful bank president, the champion athlete, the homemaker, the famous, the unknown, every human being, you, I, die. While all acknowledge the certainty of their eventual demise, few think about death until they are faced with it. The simple fact of death is not news to anyone, yet the reality of its impending occurrence is ignored by virtually every living person. The very nature of human life denies death and shrouds it in the cloak of future events, events that are not yet real and need not be dealt with in the present. Living is too important and time consuming to be concerned with mortality. The fact that you are moving steadily toward your death is most likely, and literally, to be the last thing on your mind.

Observing the inevitable death of every creature that inhabits the earth, we may have a recurrent feeling that death is the end. On the other hand, it is virtually inconceivable to us that all we are, all we have been, all we will be, may be rendered void in that moment of death. It goes against human nature to visualize the effective destruction of our past, present, and future, which may accompany death without existence beyond death. Yet if each human being does cease to exist, then all human beings are, or in the case of generations yet unborn will be, waiting their turn to cease existing. If each and every human being ceases to be, then the feeling of continuity that pervades the human race may be false (please note we do not believe that life is in fact destroyed by physical death).

In their arguments for humanism, existentialism, etc., philosophers have spent lifetimes trying to construct a difference between the apparent continuity of humankind, and the periodic death of individual humans. Most of us think of our ancestors as a link to the past, and our children as a link to the future, yet if we do not survive the grave each generation may die an isolated death that mocks any assertion that humankind has a continuing existence apart from its individual members. If each person's death results in their no longer existing, then no manner of historical recording, social progression, or other remembrance in the minds of those whose time to die is yet to come, can in any way affect, preserve, or make any difference whatsoever to those who no longer are. No one will survive to remember. If each of us ceases to be, then your life may have no meaning and your choices may make no difference.

We admit that this logic seems counter intuitive, and even wrong, but if we are willing to dissociate ourselves from the incredible biologic urge for self-preservation, both of the individual and the species, and are willing to apply purely objective reasoning, the logical conclusions, while discomforting, are perhaps inevitable (there are several possible logical loopholes which we discuss below that might give permanent meaning and value to a finite physical life). This is a very difficult conclusion to accept, it goes against our intuitive feelings about the continuity of human life, and against our assumptions that individual physical lives have some kind of meaning and value.

Yet if we are little more than doomed animals, our intuitive feeling of meaning and value would not be surprising. From the very beginning, to assure survival of any species, evolution would certainly have instilled in living creatures the feeling that there is a reason for them to exist, a reason for them to crawl out of the ocean and build cities. If there is no life after death, and our lives are in fact consumed by "nothing", it is no wonder that our genetic heritage argues so strongly against that possibility.

Because it is so difficult to accept, we will consider our conclusion in more detail. It seems logical to assume that if each person's consciousness is the product of their physical bodies, then individual physical consciousness exists only during that person's physical life on earth. If each of our physical lives proceeds from birth to death, then the consequence of each person's death necessarily follows their death. Who can be affected by that death? Certainly those who survive may be affected, but here is the "problem", the death cannot be of any consequence to the purely physical human being who no longer exists! The moment before the death of a human being it can be said that their impending death affects them, but the very moment after the person dies he or she is no longer around to be affected!

Most agree that cause and effect, action and consequence, occur in a fixed order, the former always "preceding" the latter. Let us assume, for example, that a comet collides with the Earth at some time in the future before humans have colonized space. Assume further that all life on Earth is annihilated by the collision. It is very hard to accept, but if consciousness, our mind, is nothing more than physical phenomena, if there is no non-physical continuation of life after death, then the most logical conclusion is that the complete annihilation of humankind is of absolutely no consequence to humankind! While the words may sound bizarre and counter intuitive, in fact they may not be. The moment after the total destruction of humankind it can be said with some certainty that the destruction of humankind had no effect whatsoever on humankind simply because humankind no longer exists to be affected.

If you accept that time has direction (we believe that even absent a "fundamental time", all events follow a causal, sequential, chain), then cause and effect, action and consequence, occur in a fixed order, the former always preceding the latter. Keeping that in mind, the idea that after the total destruction of humankind there would be no one left to be affected should not seem as bizarre. Assuming that one event will always precede another event in order of occurrence, if the event that is called the death of a human being is equivalent to the physical annihilation of that human being, the consequence of that event necessarily follows the event. If there is a causal sequence to events, then the annihilation cannot be of any consequence to a human being who no longer exists (note that our logic may be questioned by those who think we live in some kind of a block universe, we will discuss this later).

Again, the moment before the destruction of humankind perhaps it could be said that the impending destruction affects humankind, but the very moment after humankind is destroyed there is absolutely no humankind left to be affected. Assume that the comet annihilates humankind at 12:00 noon, the consequence of that destruction occurs at 12:00 noon PLUS a moment in time, and at 12:00 noon plus the moment in time there is no humankind left to be affected. Indeed, there is no humankind around that is conscious of the fact that the comet struck the earth!

The same logic applies to the history of individuals not visited by a catastrophic event. If you believe that each human being is nothing more than an individual physical entity, and therefore that there is no life after death, then at the time of their death each human being experiences the identical individual annihilation that all humankind would experience together if the earth and its inhabitants were simultaneously "destroyed". If a human being dies at 12:00 noon, and there is no life after death, at 12:01 they are not "around" to be affected by their death.

If an individual named Bill dies at 12:00 noon, at 12:01 Bill no longer exists to be affected by his death. If Bill is a purely physical entity that does not survive death, after 12:00 noon (i.e. - after completion of the sequence of causal events that precede Bill's death) you could search the entire universe for Bill and you would not find him (some readers are probably thinking that Bill continues to exist as his worldline in a block universe even after his physical death, we will also discuss that later). Bill's death occurs at precisely 12:00 noon. Not minutes, or even moments, later. If there is no life after death, the very moment after the event known as Bill's death, Bill no longer exists. After 12:00 noon Bill cannot be affected by anything, including his death.

The logic goes even further. If you do not believe that human consciousness continues to exist after physical death, then death not only annihilates each individual's present and future, but also annihilates their past. Most people would agree that for an object to have a present and a future the object must exist. Yet many would make the distinction that while an object cannot have a present and a future if it does not exist, it somehow can have a past. It is clear that the present and future

16

of an object are bound to the existence of the object, but so too is the object's past. Much of the problem lies in the use of the words past, present, and future both to describe that which is part of an object (a "past" which belongs to the object, like a person's memories that "belong" to the living individual from birth to death), and to describe the existence of the object from a third party's view (a "past" which is a chronological description of an object, like a photo album containing a lifetime collection of pictures of an individual who has died).

It is a misconception to equate the fact that there is a "history" of all beings or objects which is set in the "past", with the statement that a being or object that no longer exists has a "past". The first idea simply says that the being or object existed over a finite period that is apparent to those who currently exist. The extension of the concept of such a history to the idea that somehow the object or being that no longer exists still possesses a "past" confuses the distinction these two words can convey.

Once an object or being no longer exists it obviously has no present or future, similarly the object has no past. While it may be difficult to accept, a mountain that no longer exists has no past, present, or future for the simple reason that there is no such mountain. There is a current history of a mountain that once existed, but there is no mountain we can point to and describe the "past" of. This is far more than semantics. A person who lived a thousand years ago had a historic life that those who are alive can be conscious of, but the person no longer has a past that is their past, which they can be conscious of.

The English language lacks the words that would make it easy to convey the difference between a "history" set in the past that is the sum of all lifetimes, and a "past" that is unique to and dependent on the existence of an individual life. Perhaps humankind has avoided the discomforting possibility of "finite pasts" by not distinguishing them from the infinite. Perhaps the majority simply do not accept the possibility of the perpetual annihilation of human beings.

Admittedly, our conclusions about physical death are totally opposite to our "common sense" understanding of life. Virtually everyone is certain, for example, that if they are eleven years old now, and therefore have already experienced their tenth birthday, nothing can take away from them the past experience of being ten years old. It is this assumption, that our past somehow exists forever, that is at the heart of all humanistic belief systems. Indeed, belief in some kind of physical persistence of a human being's past is the only rational argument for the universal humanistic conclusion that even if physical death is the end, living a "good life" gives meaning and value to human existence. However, as we have just discussed, there is a problem with the humanist's view.

Humanist philosophers seem to accept that human consciousness is purely physical in nature and acknowledge the end of consciousness at physical death. Yet almost all modern humanist philosophers tell us that a finite life can have meaning and value. The problem lies in failure to accept the rational and logical possible consequences for each human being if individual consciousness ceases to exist on the physical death of the mind and body. Humanist philosophers either ignore or misunderstand what the future may hold for us after physical death if we are nothing more than physical beings. They fail to recognize that humanist beliefs may be nothing more than modern myths.

There are many arguments that purport to counter our logic, including assertions that a person's life before physical death has "existential" meaning (we use "existential" in the sense of having meaning and purpose "in and of itself"). Yet the alternative arguments are set in the time before death, within the causal sequence of events that precede death. Every mainstream humanistic theory is based on the biophysics of existence before physical death. We believe that none of the arguments adequately address the period after death (perhaps with the possible exception suggested by modern physics that is discussed below), and therefore none answer the question of how a person who no longer exists can be conscious of, and be said to possess, a past, a present, or a future?

What Does Science Say?

What does science have to say about all this? We need to recognize that the very difficult conclusions we reach in this section are not necessarily supported by conventional interpretations of general relativity and quantum mechanics. The current understanding that human beings have of the physical universe is fundamentally incomplete. Early concepts of space and time as physical entities would seem to be fully consistent with our analysis. However, modern physics tells us that the universe is much more complex than it was once thought to be. At the start of the third millennium, it is generally accepted that we exist in some kind of four dimensional "space-time". The mathematician Hermann Minkowski, who helped formalize the math of space-time, said "...henceforth, space by itself, and time by itself, have vanished into the merest shadows and only a kind of blend of the two exists in its own right."

Space-time is essentially the history of the entire universe, containing every "event" that ever happens. A "worldline" is the history of an object in "space-time". Each point on the worldline of a human being is generally thought to be a real physical event that represents a unique sequential moment in the life of that individual, from birth to death. Conventional wisdom is that the worldline of a human being is the "human being", so that human life is in some real sense a permanent part of space-time. If so, perhaps we have a permanent physical past that is etched in the fabric of space-time.

To see why we do not believe that science provides us with a physical past, we need to look at two interpretations of cosmologic theories and one other possibility (there are many variations but the three we discuss illustrate the most important viewpoints). The first possible interpretation, the one that we strongly favor, brings into question the very nature of space-time. At first glance, the concept of a permanent physical space-time, a block universe, seems to imply that human beings have a permanent physical past, present, and future. Most people assume that the math of space-time describes a permanent physical reality that surrounds us, a very real, very physical, space-time in which we exist. This may or may not be the case.

The limited number of physicists who understand the incredibly difficult math realize that the theory of general relativity tells us that the universe may be completely described without using a "fundamental temporal variable", without even defining what we call "time". The time we measure on a stopwatch that we use to clock a foot race is derived from comparing the motion of the runner from the starting line to the finish line with the motion of the hand rotating around the face of the watch. The time on the stopwatch may not be, as Newton thought, a fundamental quantity in nature, rather it may be nothing more than a comparison of the motion of the person running down the track relative to the motion of the hands of the stopwatch. Therefore, we may be justified in concluding that "time" is derived from relative motion, but that relative motion does not require the passage of time. It may be true that "fundamental time" simply does not exist.

This is a shocking idea for human beings who are confronted with the ticking away of years, days, hours, and seconds. Yet if you think about it, a year is nothing more than the relative motion of the earth going around the sun, a day is the relative motion of the earth rotating around its axis, an hour is a fraction of the motion we call a day measured by a quartz "moving" in a watch, a second is very close to the relative motion of a beating heart. We don't expect to convince you in a few paragraphs that time is an illusion, it took years of reading and thought for us to reach that conclusion, but we do want you to recognize that there is a strong possibility that fundamental time does not exist. If this is a correct interpretation of general relativity, it can lead to the conclusion that there is no fundamental temporality of any kind associated with our universe.

There are serious objections to this line of thought. In its popular forms, the other 20th century revolution in physics, quantum mechanics, incorporates a fundamental temporal variable. Some scientists believe that general relativity will be found to be incomplete, and that quantum mechanics tells us that time does in fact exist. Other physicists agree that the universe lacks a fundamental temporal variable by which the universe evolves, yet they also believe that in some very real sense the universe exhibits fundamental "temporality". None-the-less, there are a few respected physicists who believe that we should accept what general relativity is telling us, that there is no fundamental temporal variable in the universe, and find a way to modify quantum mechanics to eliminate "time" and perhaps even "temporality" from quantum theory. Given the success of general relativity in predicting experimental results we believe that this is the correct approach. We are convinced that if and when physicists discover a broad model that incorporates both relativity and quantum theories, what is usually called a theory of quantum gravity, it will not have any kind of fundamental temporal variable associated with it and we will find that the universe is fundamentally "atemporal" in nature.

If the theory of general relativity is in fact part of the illusive theory of quantum gravity, and if we do in fact live in an "atemporal" universe then it is indeed quite possible that physical events in our lives either exist, or do not exist. The statement that a point on a worldline exists in the universe may be false, true, false, with no sense that "false" is "before" or "after" true! If so, then it may be quite literally true that your tenth birthday does not exist, does exist, does not exist in the universe. Perhaps you believe that your tenth birthday is a permanent part of your past only because it is part of your current memories, not because it exists in some kind of permanent physical space-time. Note that our view is what philosophers call "extreme presentism", at the start of the third millennium it has been rejected, or at least declared to be unsupported by existing theories, by many but not all scientists. None-the-less, some scientists believe that adopting some form of presentism is the correct way to understand our physical universe.

If we live in an essentially "atemporal" universe where there is state evolution but no "time", and if there is no non-physical existence after death, then we believe that physical death consumes each human being's physical past, present, and future. This is very difficult to understand and accept, yet the idea that there is no fundamental temporality and that this fact leads to the annihilation of our physical past, appears to us to be the correct interpretation of our physical universe. However, our conclusions are based on very complex and controversial relativistic and quantum science, we think we are right but we may be wrong.

The reason that we cannot be more certain that our conclusions are correct is simply because no one knows what physics will look like if and when relativity and quantum theories are united. Furthermore, there is no way to tell how long it will take to find answers to the basic questions raised by modern physics. Indeed, it is quite possible that we will never know the answers to many of our most fundamental questions. We believe that the universe is essentially atemporal, and that physical death annihilates our physical (but not any non-physical) past, present, and future, but we may simply be wrong.

OK, let's say that you are unwilling to even think about "time" not existing, would the existence of "time" or at least "fundamental temporality" restore a meaningful physical past to your life? The second possibility we will look at is based on the fact that most popular interpretations of modern physics suggest that the physical existence of each human being somehow persists in space-time in the form of the individual's "worldline". Classical interpretations often say that an object is the entire worldline of that object, or that a human being is his or her worldline, but they do not really explain what is meant by this. However, they almost universally conclude that each event in a human being's life exists as an event in space-time, so that if we could observe the point on a worldline that is the tenth birthday of someone who is now twenty years old we would see that person experiencing their tenth birthday. We would not see a "copy", or a "repeat", of the particular day, we would see the person's tenth birthday as it is occurring, period!

It would seem that this characteristic of all popular space-time theories leaves us without tools for building a rational model of a universe that contains a "conscious" worldline that is the "me" reading this book. Rather it tells us that there is, and always will be, a set of unique "me's" that somehow exist in space-time at every single event on my worldline. "Me" on my tenth, twentieth, thirtieth birthdays and all the days in-between. We might want to say that I am the sum of all the points, yet the assertion that a human being is his or her entire worldline, from birth to death, does not appear to be consistent with the general consensus that every event along a worldline has a singular existence that cannot be preferred over any other event on that worldline.

The theory of relativity tells us that all of the laws of physics are the same for every inertial observer. If we live in a fully relational, relativistic universe, we simply cannot prefer observations made in the inertial frame of reference of one observer over observations made in the inertial frame of reference of any other observer, no matter where they may be "located" in space-time. A consequence of this fact is that for one observer your tenth birthday occurs before your eleventh birthday, while for another (spatially separated) observer your eleventh birthday occurs before your tenth! Relativity tells us that both observers are 100% correct in their observations (this is one of many reasons we prefer an atemporal model of our physical universe). The cosmos is a very strange place indeed!

Classic interpretations imply that each individual exists as discrete human consciousness in the billions of discrete events located at every point along that individual's worldline. Some physicists describe this by saying that there are many "now's"; others say there are billions of approximate "isomorphs" of "me"; many claim there are billions of other worlds in which various versions of "me" co-exist; etc. It seems reasonable to conclude that modern physics tells us that if time exists, literally billions of discrete, very real, versions of each of us occupy space-time!

This may seem like science fiction, yet surveys of theoretical physicists and cosmologists confirm that many if not most believe we must adopt some form of many-worlds, multiple existence, theory. Remember, this is current accepted thought and not speculative ideas. If there really are an infinite number of parallel universes (which we do not believe is true), or if there is a "me" that exists on my worldline for every event in my physical life, then there is no singular physical "me". Rather there are billions of isolated "me's" either lying along my worldline or stuck somewhere in totally isolated universes.

If the scientists are correct, it would seem to be impossible to find meaning and value for a singular "me" in the collective existence of each of the billions of instances of individual consciousness, no single one of which is the "me" who can live a meaningful life. All of the popular interpretations of relativistic and quantum theories lead us to the same conclusion, if you do not have a singular permanent existence your life has no meaning and your choices make no difference to "you", simply because there is no single physical "you" that exists before or after physical death (please remember, we believe that life has meaning and value).

You may be wondering what the difference is in an atemporal and a block universe? If you compare an atemporal universe with a block universe, similarities quickly appear. On the website, The Astronomy Café, Dr. Sten Odenwald describes the key characteristic of a block universe: "Space-time does not evolve, it simply exists. When we examine a particular object from the standpoint of its space-time representation, every particle is located along its world-line... Once you determine the complete world line of a particle from the forces acting upon it, you have 'solved' for its complete history. This world-line does not change with time, but simply exists as a timeless object. Similarly, in general relativity, when you solve equations for the shape of space-time, this shape does not change in time, but exists as a complete timeless object..." So if a block and an atemporal universe are both "timeless" objects, why does it matter which theory is correct? Do not both contain many "me's", one at each point on the bundle of worldlines that is "me". If in an atemporal universe we do not have state evolution as a result of the passage of time, how can we say that human beings progress from birth to death?

There are a couple possibilities. The math behind something called symplectic mechanics allows us to have a kind of mechanical evolution in an atemporal universe which is essentially the result of sequential cause and effect, like a row of dominoes falling when the first one is pushed. This progression of events does not require the existence of a fundamental temporal variable. This is one possibility, but we do not know what really happens in the universe. There are more exotic mechanisms for state evolution in atemporal models, including asymmetric quantum state evolution, which suggest that there may be change in an atemporal universe that would not be allowed in a block universe.

It seems that science suggests there may be several ways objects in an atemporal universe might evolve utilizing some mechanism that is consistent with our conclusion that we exist in the "present" and not the past or future. If this is true then our conclusions that our past, present and future being annihilated by physical death are supported by an atemporal model. On the other hand, it is also possible that an atemporal universe is not distinguishable from a block universe. If that is true, then we are once again confronted by the prospect of many "me's". Both possibilities would seem to leave us without a singular consciousness which preserves and gives meaning to our past, present, and future.

There is a third possibility, that the intuitive feeling human beings have that their physical past cannot change or be lost is based on some real, yet unknown, physical model of our universe. As we have said, virtually everyone is certain that if they are eleven years old they have already experienced their tenth year of life, and that nothing can take from them the past experience of being ten years old. The intuitive feeling is very strong that our physical life makes a positive or negative contribution to human existence, and that our physical life is a permanent part of the physical universe. Perhaps there is some single physical consciousness that incorporates all of the events along our worldline, and that preserves our physical past, present, and future.

We cannot rule out this possibility, if for no other reason than the fact that it is theoretically impossible to prove a negative. In other words, we might be able to prove that physical consciousness after death exists in the universe by observing it, but we can never prove that physical consciousness or some other form of existential meaning does not exist after death because we have not observed it. Indeed, the very fact that human beings exist in our universe argues strongly for existential meaning and purpose. If we have a physical existence that has existential meaning then the billions of people who intuitively believe that every day, every moment, of their lives has purpose and value are absolutely right.

Yet if we are to believe that there may be some kind of physical existence that survives physical death, then it would seem that we would need to accept that there is some unique physical consciousness that is "me", that somehow incorporates all of the conscious events of my life, and that is somehow not dependent on the physical existence of my biologic body. While current interpretations of theories do not rule out the possibility of a perpetual individual physical consciousness, there is no known method that is both rational and realistic (i.e.- a theory that appears capable of modeling physical reality), to construct a physical (as opposed to a non-physical) model that preserves the singular human physical consciousness of an individual after the physical death of that person.

Modern theories suggest the possibility that multiple instances of a physical "me" exist in space-time, but they do not tell us how to unite all of those instances into a single physical "me" whose consciousness spans space-time. Indeed, current interpretations of quantum superposition seem to deny the possibility of a "single" reality. If human beings do not have some kind of singular existence after physical death, we are again faced with the question how life can have meaning to someone who no longer exists. Einstein only briefly addressed physical (not non-physical) existence when he said "An individual who should survive his physical death is also beyond my comprehension..."

While we can visualize and accept a "non-physical consciousness" that survives physical death, we are unable to have any confidence in the existence of a singular "physical consciousness" or other form of existential meaning based on finite physical existence that survives the physical death of a human being. We may be wrong. Almost every philosopher and scientist, in fact almost all of the billions of human beings

25

who live on this earth, believe that physical life has existential meaning and purpose. We can say that after many, many years of thought we are convinced that any attempt to construct a model of permanent physical consciousness and/or existential meaning for human beings who no longer exist, does more damage to the centuries of accumulated scientific knowledge than does the acceptance of the possibility that a permanent non-physical consciousness may exist.

In coming out of the dark ages human beings have made enormous intellectual leaps in philosophy and science, so much so that many now believe we understand how life works. We need to recognize the fact that when future generations look back at twenty-first century science it will seem as primitive to them as alchemy does to us and they will be rightly amazed at our lack of understanding of our existence. There are thought experiments that might provide a theoretical foundation for existential consciousness and might give meaning to our lives in ways that we cannot imagine. Yet at this point the speculative ideas being proposed are little more than science fiction, there is no objective reason to believe that any of them will be found to be true.

We have concluded, rightly or wrongly, that no current, or reasonably foreseeable, rational theory provides us with a singular physical consciousness or other existential existence so that after my physical death a single physical "me" continues to exist in my physical "past". We have said that if we do not have a singular physical or non-physical consciousness that continues to exist after physical death, then those who believe in nihilism are probably correct, and some type of "nihilistic" void awaits all of us. It may be a true void, like the void that preceded our birth, or it may be a very strange void where billions of "me" merely co-exist. Whatever physical form it might take, it would seem to satisfy the definition of a "meaningless" void.

A moment's comment on those who believe they may be able to physically perpetuate themselves through cryogenics, cloning, brain-computer singularities, etc. If theories that predict endless cycles of expansion and contraction of our universe are correct, nothing physical can survive beyond the next collapse of the universe a few billion years from today. While that may seem absurdly far away, your great, great, great (to the 100th. power), grand-clone would find it frightfully real when the time came for the collapse, a distant time from now which like all imaginable time is but a second in eternity.

On the other hand, if we live in a constantly expanding universe, our universe will eventually return to a state of uniformly high entropy. It is generally accepted that in the very distant future, as entropy increases, the cosmos will become a hostile environment in which physical life cannot be sustained. There is no cosmologic model that we know of that offers any hope for a perpetual, physical, human existence.

Even if in some unknown manner multiple clones could survive in an ever-expanding universe, the idea that they are perpetual extensions of their donor seems less than credible. Such a perpetual physical presence seems to be more like an endless path of meaningless individual moments experienced by many me's, than a continuous meaningful existence. Furthermore, if there is no life after death, it would make no difference if an individual (cloned, merged with a machine, or otherwise) continued to exist, or "died" in one hundred years or in one billion years, because "death" would annihilate the individual's past, present, and future (we discuss this in the next chapters).

You Can't Think About Nothing

Even though we are convinced that physical death is not the end of your existence, if it is the end should you be frightened by the certainty of your demise? If indeed you cease to exist, you need not fear death, for after your death you will feel neither pain, nor pleasure, nor peace, nor torment. "You" will no longer exist, therefore "you" will feel nothing. The resulting void is just that, a complete and total void.

There would be nothing to fear, for there will be no one to experience anything negative. There would be nothing to look forward to, for there will be no one to experience anything positive. The only way you can visualize what is usually called a "nihilistic" death is to picture yourself after death as being in the same state you were in before birth (of course you were not really in any state at all). Such a fate would leave nothing to be feared.

Philosophers often speak of the void that would follow physical death without life after death as the abyss, the unknown, the approaching void, etc. All of these suggest that we are on a journey to a "place" which lies at the end of our physical lifetimes. If on our death we cease to exist, this idea that we are traveling to our ultimate destiny is false. We are not traveling to an abyss, the void, or the unknown, for these words suggest that we are moving toward something. We recognize the seeming absurdity of the language, yet if on our death we cease to exist, then "nothing" totally consumes us.

We can speak of "nothing" being in an empty room. But that is not correct because the room has dimensions and is filled with empty space. We might say that the room itself does not exist, therefore there is nothing. Yet what we are really saying is that the room does not exist within the bounded space in which we exist, which is "something". We cannot fully comprehend a room which because it is "nothing", does not exist anywhere, anytime.

This is the heart of the problem, we cannot in any way whatsoever understand or visualize "nothing". When we think about "nothing" we turn it into "something" that can be thought about. The moment we attempt to comprehend or visualize "nothing", we interject something into "nothing", preventing us from reaching our goal. The only way we can answer the question "what is nothing?" is to answer it by not asking it, for if we ask the question we destroy the answer.

Most people fail to recognize the fact that "something" simply cannot comprehend "nothing". If we are no more than physical beings, and if "nothing" follows our physical death, then at the moment of our physical death, "nothing". The possibility of "nothing" absolutely frees us from any concern we may have about a physical life that has an end and demands that we live for the possibility, however slight we may believe it to be, that there is "something". We discuss why this is true in the next chapter.

Afraid of Nothing?

What should our response be to all of this? We strongly believe that there is absolutely no reason not to live for the possibility that life has meaning and value. We think we are right about the transitory nature of physical consciousness, but we may be totally wrong. If we are wrong, if each of us has a singular physical consciousness that somehow survives physical death, or if there is some other form of existential existence that gives meaning and purpose to our physical lives, then our life may have meaning and value even if there is no non-physical life after death. We will not pursue this possibility, yet you should recognize that it might, or might not, exist.

A brief comment on the word possible. Saying something may be possible is misleading in the case of mutually exclusive options. When we say there is a possibility that our conclusions are wrong, or a possibility that there is no non-physical life after death, or a possibility that there is existential meaning without a non-physical life after death, we are talking about facts that are either true or false. Our conclusions are right, or they are wrong, either there is a non-physical life after death or there is no non-physical life after death, either there is existential meaning absent a non-physical afterlife or there is not. If life has no meaning without a non-physical existence after physical death, and there is no life after physical death, then there is no "possibility" of existential meaning. If there is existential meaning to life without non-physical existence after death, then the possibility of existential meaning exists and always has existed.

If in fact there is no non-physical life after death, then there is no possibility of a non-physical life after death and such a possibility never existed. Yet if there is a non-physical life after death then the possibility, indeed the actuality, of life after death exists and always has existed. Whenever you see the word possible, and similar words like might or may, remember that if something does not and cannot exist, then that something is never possible (the probability is zero). If something can exist, then that something represents an actual possibility.

If we are right, if our consciousness and existential physical being do not survive physical death, our death may mark the end of our existence. Yet if our physical consciousness dies, it is still quite possible that

31

we will not face a "nihilistic" death. Perhaps we have a non-physical consciousness that survives physical death, and that gives meaning and value to our lives. We consider this possibility in more detail as we search for a reason for living.

Beyond the human desire for meaning in life, we would suggest that the logical consequences of what philosophers call a nihilistic death require the search for alternatives to nihilism. Those who believe that the nihilistic void is approaching are, by the very nature of their humanity, required to search for something to believe in other than the void. While it appears to be impossible to scientifically prove that life has meaning and value, it is equally impossible to prove that life has no meaning and value. No matter what the person who concludes that life is meaningless believes to be true now or at any other particular time in their life, the possibility always exists that he or she may eventually find true meaning and value.

The following is very hard to explain and may take several readings and a great deal of effort to understand. The limits of human comprehension make it extremely difficult to recognize the fact that if there is a nihilistic void after physical death, then there is absolutely no reason at all to think about the "nothing" that may follow physical life. Nothing cannot affect our physical lives, either positively or negatively. It cannot be a part of our existence, it cannot be a part of our thoughts, it is "nothing".

If after our physical death there is "nothing" then when we die we will not experience calm or peace or pain or distress, we will not experience anything because we will not exist. "Nothing" will not relieve us of anything simply because there will be no one to experience relief, there will be no "you" who can feel the absence of pain. You will not remember the good times or the horrific events in your life. We need to accept the difficult but essential point, if nothing follows physical death then there is no peaceful sleep because no one exists who can sleep, there are no nightmares because there is no one to dream. All will be as if it never was.

If you live five years in excruciating pain and there is nothing after physical death, then when you die the pain does not "end", it is as if those five years never happened. If you live fifty years in excruciating pain and there is nothing after physical death, then when you die the pain does not "end", it is as if those fifty years never happened. If there is nothing after physical death, you gain nothing if your physical pain lasts only five instead of fifty years, there is no difference. In both cases on the day of your death the excruciating pain does not "end", it is as if the pain never was.

There is a profound difference between pain which ends and pain which never was. It may seem that anything which results in pain being as if it never happened is an end to the pain we are suffering, but that is not a true description of the "reality" of not existing, of "nothing". Take the time to really think about the difference, you will eventually realize that if on our physical death our past is consumed by nothing, it is no worse to suffer fifty years of pain than suffer five years. If in fact there is nothing after physical death, then if you live one minute, or 20 or 30 or 40 or 50 more years, all the horrors in your past, present, and future will be "consumed" by nothing. This is not the same as saying that we find "peace" in a nihilistic death, we find "nothing". All will be as if it never was.

Similarly, if you live a long and comfortable life filled with personal accomplishments, and there is nothing after physical death, then on your physical death "nothing". If there is nothing after physical death you will have no past. It will be as if you were never born, as if you never existed. All will be as if it never was.

If there is nothing after physical death, there can be absolutely no benefit to a shorter life, no logical reason to want physical life to end. Even though it may seem absurd, if we do not exist after our physical death we have no reason to fear, or avoid, five years or fifty years of the most horrible pain. The all-consuming nature of the "nothing" that may follow physical death is what human beings find almost impossible to comprehend. Yet understanding the possibility of "something", life after physical death or existential meaning to physical life, and the freedom of "nothing" if we are wrong, allows us to live as long and as good a physical life as possible.

If you are living a pleasant life your initial response to the possibility of "nothing" may be that it is frightening, or if you are suffering it may feel somehow comforting, both thoughts are totally, unquestionably, wrong. If on our physical death there is nothing, then there is no rational or logical reason to think about physical death as fearful or peaceful. If there is nothing after physical death then the experience of physical death (perhaps it is better to say the experience that never happens) is the same if it occurs in one day or one year or one hundred years, during a period of great joy or great pain. There would be "nothing" in your future to look forward to, there would be "nothing" in your future to fear.

If you really understand what this means, you recognize that the possibility of nothing allows us to endure all the physical and emotional pain we experience no matter how horrific, and to live the most positive life we can with the hope that there is a non-physical life after our death. It is very important to recognize that nihilism can never lead to suicide, for nihilism tells us that if we do in fact live in a nihilistic world, nothing that happens in our lives, no matter how painful it is and how badly we may feel about it at the time, has any "real" consequence at all.

If there is nothing after death, then it makes no difference to you if your life was filled with pain or pleasure, because you will not exist to feel pain or pleasure. Yet if there is an existence after death, then by having chosen to endure physical pain and chosen to live the most positive physical life you can, you may find after your physical death that memories of even the worst pain are overwhelmed by "joy" and "disappear". If there is an existence after physical death then enduring a lifetime of physical and emotional pain may result in a timeless eternity of peace and happiness. If there is an existence after death, and you choose suicide, you may be rejecting that peace and happiness.

The possibility of nothing leaves you absolutely free to live a life filled with both pain and joy, knowing that if you live in a meaningless world the pain will be as if it never was. Terminating life never brings release from pain, rather it may destroy the possibility of a meaningful, perhaps joyful, non-physical life. If there is an existence after death, and you choose suicide, you may be rejecting that peace and happiness. We are absolutely convinced that the philosophical neutrality that nihilism demands means that nihilism never suggests or in any way supports suicide as an option for any human being.

If you believe that suicide is an option, you totally misunderstand what you have read, you do not comprehend what it means to say that "nothing" may consume your past, present, and future. You do not understand what it means to say that all will be as if it never was. You need to reread the last four chapters until you understand that nihilism renders false all arguments for suicide.

It is absolutely, undeniably, true that we do not know and understand the fundamental nature of our universe and our existence, and that we may in fact not live in a nihilistic world. We are a small part of the whole. Unless the answer is revealed to us by the whole, we can never know during our physical lives what really happens when our physical life ends. Life may have physical or non-physical meaning and value right now that we do not, and perhaps cannot during our physical lives, recognize and understand. It is absolutely, undeniably, true that since nihilism may be wrong, there can never be any reason to terminate our life, risk the negative consequences, and abandon the possible positive benefits of living a meaningful life.

There is no reason to be a nihilist, no reason to believe that life has no meaning and purpose. If we live in a nihilistic world, if life does end at death, it makes no difference what we believe or do about nihilism because we cannot alter the void. Yet if nihilism is not correct, then belief and/or faith in that which offers a reason for living is essential to our existence. If because we believe nihilism is correct we accept the void, and we are wrong, then we have doomed ourselves. If you believe that the humanistic belief that there is no life after death may lead to the nihilistic conclusion that the "void" will consume past, present, and future, then to escape the quicksand of nihilistic time you must search for alternatives that provide a reason for living.

There is no reason at all to reject the possibility that each of us has some kind of permanent physical or non-physical consciousness. There is no reason at all to reject the possibility that each of our lives has existential meaning and purpose even if there is no life after death. There is no reason whatsoever not to search for an alternative to nihilism, to explore the possibility of a permanent physical or non-physical consciousness, to seek existential meaning and purpose in our lives, to consider the possibility of a non-physical existence after physical death, to search for a reason for living. There is absolutely no reason whatsoever not to live for the possibility, however remote you may believe it to be, that you can make choices now that will lead you to a positive life that has meaning and value. [Again, if you find yourself distressed or depressed by our conclusions please read the Appendix – Distress & Depression.]

Is That All There Is?

If it is true that your existence ends with physical death, does that mean that your life is meaningless? As we have said, the answer is "probably" (but not "certainly") yes. Therefore, is it true that your life has no meaning? The answer is a qualified no. If we are somehow more than our physical bodies, if we can exist beyond and apart from those bodies, then perhaps each of us survives physical death and continues to exist, in some manner and form, beyond the grave. If you are, or you become through living, a unique individual who possesses the ability to engage in rational thought and exercise freedom of choice transcending biological processes of determinism, perhaps you have an existence beyond your physical mind and body, perhaps not.

Since the dawn of recorded history people have thought and written about existence beyond physical death. Some have suggested that extra sensory perception, premonitions, unexplained knowledge of past events, along with other similar and possibly real phenomena, are part of the world beyond death, perhaps so, perhaps not. Perhaps the unique being which each of us is, the present existence that makes your choices and your life yours alone, exists now and after your death in a realm beyond the physical, perhaps not. Perhaps that which you are survives like energy in a dimension coexistent with the physical world but beyond the constraints of space, motion, and time, perhaps not. Perhaps each of us continues to exist in a manner and fashion infinitely beyond our ability to imagine, let alone comprehend, perhaps not.

A great number of people have spent vast amounts of time and effort studying all manner of phenomena outside everyday experiences. Many, most, or even all "inexplicable" events may be explained by future generations of scientists. The most amazing phenomena are not the dramatic events often attributed to the supernatural, events which could as easily as not be emotional illusions or the consequence of known or unknown physical laws. What are amazing to us are simple occurrences that defy probability. We have all experienced, and therefore witnessed, baffling events that leave one with a feeling that their explanation may lie outside the realm of natural science.

For example, most of us have thought about someone we have not seen for years, only to bump into them a few minutes later. Even more amazing are instances that may occur when we are facing major events in our lives, when we are in some way confronted by someone or something that leads us toward a "better" choice. When faced with such occurrences, we have often found ourselves with an intuitive feeling that they are in some non-physical sense planned, perhaps so, perhaps not.

We have paid a great deal of attention to the kind of occurrences that are classified by scientists as "amazing coincidences". While most can be accepted as coincidental, some appear to be one in a million events that happen with such regularity that the odds against them being merely coincidental are incredibly large. It is impossible for us, in good conscience, to dismiss them as being nothing more than random events. Many appear to be objective phenomena, well suited to empirical study, that statistically support the conclusion that they are not the result of chance.

We have little difficulty accepting that there are events which are in fact controlled by forces beyond our present knowledge. Indeed, we are convinced that there is a non-physical explanation for many events. If they are true phenomena, and not products of the mind, their very existence strongly suggests that there is a world which is quite real lying somewhere beyond normal human perception. A brief glance at, a fleeting contact with, what may be the world beyond the one in which we live gives a shocking reality to what we academically speculate about, or even faithfully believe in.

Though we may profess to believe in that which we cannot see, we may also find ourselves surprised when our beliefs appear to be true. Possible contact with a world beyond human perception gives us a startling realization that we may be eternally subject to forces absolutely beyond our control and leaves us with a chilling or hopeful feeling (depending on your view of your prospects if eternity exists) that death will not be an eternal sleep. None-the-less, no matter how convincing at the moment, a belief that we may have glimpsed the world beyond is diluted over time. The human mind's natural presumption is against out of the ordinary observations that, by definition, provide infrequent reinforcement of beliefs.

Of course, it may be true that "supernatural" events, though perhaps of great significance to the living, are nothing more than manifestations of physical and biological processes beyond our present ability to explain, similar to early civilization's attempts to explain through myths the phenomena of fire and lightening. If so they have no significance at all to the question of our existence after physical death. Yet it may be that they are images created by the overlapping of the current world and a world you will find yourself in after death.

There are no present answers to the questions posed by what many perceive to be "metaphysical", in the sense of being non-physical, events. Our discussion deals with what the meaning and purpose of life is. As we continue you will see that the question of whether or not anyone has in fact witnessed supernatural phenomena originating from a world beyond the grave, though a question which piques curiosity, is not an essential, or perhaps even an important, one. You will see that we don't need to look for metaphysical events in our lives to understand what life is all about. The significance of such events is beyond the scope of this book and is simply not necessary to our discussion.

We will see that even if no one ever has any contact in this world with a world beyond the grave, that does not mean that such a world does not exist. We will explore in detail the possibility that we may continue to exist after death. At this point we ask that you keep an open mind about life after death. For now, please accept the possibility, however remote you may feel it is, that in some manner and fashion we continue to exist after our physical death.

The Search for Truth

If a scientist, philosopher, or anyone else tells you something is true, and in fact it is not true, it is not true. To say something is true does not make it true. Even though you are told something is true, if it is not true it is simply not true. On the other hand, if something is true it is true, even if you are told or believe that it is not.

If something is true or false, it is true or false whether we believe it to be true or false, or have not thought about its truth at all. If we believe a lamp is on a table, whether we have any evidence it is or not, and the lamp is in fact on the table, then what we believe to be true is true. If we cannot determine whether or not the lamp is on the table that does not change the actual position of the lamp. Even though without evidence we cannot prove a lamp is on a table, if it is on the table then it is on the table and our belief is true. Just because we cannot prove something is true does not in any way mean it is not true. Because we cannot prove, or disprove, we continue to exist after the death of our bodies does not mean that we do not continue to exist, or that we do. If we continue to exist after our physical death, then we continue to exist, and if we do not, then we do not.

If there is no one in a forest to hear a tree fall, does the sound of the tree falling really exist? If there is no one to see a tree fall, does it really fall at all? "Does an event occur if there are no observers?" is a valid question that perhaps can be answered "yes" only if the observer not only sees the event, but also continues to exist forever beyond the time of the event. In other words, if only inanimate objects surround an event such as the turning on of a lamp, perhaps it can be said no event has occurred since nothing has been seen, heard, etc., to change. Similarly, if a living observer witnesses an event but at some later date the observer ceases to exist, what value was the observation?

Of course the argument can be made that seen or not seen photons stream from a light when it is turned on. Furthermore, it can be suggested that once seen or heard an event has in some sense "actualized". Much depends on how you define "event", but underlying the question is a troublesome perception that goes beyond semantics, a feeling that a world without permanent observers lacks anything similar to what we call "reality".

Even though we disagree, some philosophers have moved toward the view that "language" is the unique factor which gives humans the ability to think thoughts, and that language is the only thing that distinguishes us from animals. They suggest that using language, our consciousness assigns the concepts of true and false to the things and events that surround us. Some of them believe that "truth" has no meaning outside the human mind, and, therefore, in a very real sense, that "truth" does not exist as an independent reality.

We are not uncomfortable with the idea that in an inanimate universe truth may not exist, and therefore there must be an observer for truth to have meaning. However we are very uncomfortable with the suggestion that where a permanent observer does exist truth is merely a creation of that observer's consciousness. If we survive the grave, we may well have a perpetual consciousness that can observe and perhaps remember the truths which surround us. Whether or not a lamp has been observed to be on a table, if the lamp is physically sitting on a table the very existence of permanent observers who could observe the lamp may give independent meaning to the statement that it is "true" that the lamp is on the table.

If memories of human events die with each person, then events themselves become little more than transient observations made by the living. Yet if we survive the grave, it seems that we would have a continuing consciousness which recognizes a real and fundamental difference between that which is true and that which is false. For now, please accept the possibility that some things are either fundamentally "true", or not.

If we want to consider in greater detail the possibility of our continued existence after the death of our bodies, we need to be able to make statements we can believe to be true. In our quest to find some meaning in life, we must develop some method of determining "truths" which we can have a fair degree of confidence in. To do so we first need to understand what it means to be able to "prove" something, scientifically or otherwise.

Over the centuries the quest for truth has been refined into the process of scientific analysis. A brief summary of what has come to be known as the scientific method is helpful. Scientists observe what they want to study and record properties they believe to be relevant to their research. While some may have preconceived notions of what they will find, others begin the process of experimentation and observation without any idea what, if anything, they will discover. Even though they may believe they will achieve a certain result, scientists who do not approach every experiment with open minds are not scientists at all.

After gathering what they consider to be enough information about an object or event, scientists sit back, study the data, and try to combine and organize the information to discover a pattern running through it. They look for a model that not only describes what they currently observe, but that also perfectly matches past observations. The resulting descriptions of the world around them are known as theories or theorems. These in turn can be used to predict what will happen in the future under the same or similar circumstances.

Efforts to formulate theorems that describe observations would be in vain if the universe was made up of random events, occurring without reason or order, for then no one could say what will happen next. Of course, that appears not to be the case, as our universe seems to behave in a more or less ordered manner. As we have studied the cosmos in more and more detail, it seems to be true that all physical objects comprised of matter and energy (which may or may not include all aspects of human "consciousness"), from the tiniest atomic particle to the largest system, behave according to some fixed set of deterministic or probabilistic laws. These laws can be thought of as if-then statements, which describe what will happen if a certain event occurs. For example, one of the well-known results of the law of gravity is that IF an apple comes loose from the branch of a tree, THEN it will fall to earth.

For several reasons we regret using simplistic examples to make a point. Because of their simplistic nature they tend to lessen the importance of the point being made. They narrow the reader's focus from the broad, general truth of a statement to a specific, small part of the whole. Simple examples tend to be incredibly inadequate when used to illustrate complex feelings, beliefs, and ideas. Some people feel they are being talked down to or think they already understand what is being said. They risk missing the deep significance that often hides within the example. On the other hand simple examples can be used to bring a point quickly home, allowing us to bypass a good bit of background discussion and to explore at once concepts which are best understood when drawn rapidly and simultaneously into the mind. The dangers of simplistic examples can only be overcome by the reader who is aware of the shortcomings and is willing to expand in their mind the examples so that the profound will not be misunderstood to be "simple".

Back to gravity and the falling apple. The law itself basically states that objects exert a force on each other which attracts them toward one another, the strength of the attraction being related to their masses and the distance between them. The fundamental law of gravity was described by Isaac Newton after he observed that objects that are dropped fall toward earth. By repeating his experiment over and over again, by dropping object after object, Newton gained confidence what he theorized to be true was true, objects attract each other with a strength directly proportional to their masses and inversely proportional to the distance between them.

Each successful test of Newton's theory of gravity made scientists increasingly confident the theorem was correct (in fact gravity is more complex than he thought). Why should repeated successes, i.e. more and more apples falling off trees, increase the confidence of the scientists? Beyond the "common sense" feeling that repeated successes increase confidence in success, is there some "scientific" reason to be optimistic?

Enter the world of statistics. Mathematicians have long recognized that the larger the sample that is taken from a group of items the better able they are to predict what individual items are like in the group. The larger the sample the more confident they can be that a "strange" or uncharacteristic item will not be found. This is true due to the fundamental nature of the mathematics behind statistical inference. It is true no matter what the items being sampled are, so long as the sample is not biased.

For example, if you randomly sample 500 apples out of a box containing 100,000 thoroughly mixed apples, and find not a single rotten one, a mathematician can tell you with a great degree of confidence what the chances are that none of the 100,000 apples is rotten. If you sample 1,000 apples out of the 100,000 he or she can be more certain. After inspecting 10,000 apples he or she can be even more certain. If 5 rotten apples are found in a sample of 500 or 45 in a sample of 1,000 the mathematician can tell you how many rotten apples you are likely to find among the 100,000 apples. No matter what is in the box, whether it is 100,000 apples, 100,000 pencils, 100,000 transistors, 100,000 anything, so long as the items are uniformly mixed anyone can tell by drawing a random sample how many of the items in the box are likely to have one or more traits in common (i.e. color, size, shape, etc.). The bigger the sample the more accurate the prediction and the more confident the predictor.

It should be emphasized that the predictions are accurate not because of the nature of that which is being sampled, but because the mathematical relationship between the number of samples and the number of underlying items being sampled is fixed and predictable. If you draw at random four pencils from a jar containing 100 pencils, three are white, one is red, there is a certain probability that the jar contains 75% white pencils and 25% red pencils. If you draw four golf balls from a jar containing 100 golf balls, three are white, one is red, the same probability exists the jar contains 75% white golf balls and 25% red golf balls.

If the apples in our apple barrel were not uniformly mixed, and/or the sample was drawn in some organized pattern, we might get only good apples, or at least a higher number of good apples than we would otherwise. The sample would be unrepresentative of the contents of the box and useless to the mathematician. It is very, very important to realize if we take as our sample 99,999 out of 100,000 apples and find not even a single rotten one, we can be incredibly sure we are right when we predict the one apple left in the box is not rotten. None-the-less when we examine the one remaining apple it may in fact be rotten!!!!!

One final observation, there is a subtle distinction we usually miss when using statistics. If we say that there is a 40% chance of rain and a 60% chance of sunshine, and it rains, what was and is the reality of the 40% probability of sunshine? The idea that we can predict the likelihood of rain is obviously useful, but if you schedule a picnic and it rains the 60% chance of sunshine in a sense was never "real". While it may be useful to predict the probability of the event, when an event happens the possibility of it happening is 100% and the possibility of it not happening is 0%. We realize the difference in prediction and actualization, yet the fact that an event will happen if it is going to happen, and that statistics do nothing more than predict which events will occur, emphasizes the fact that fundamental forces rule both the events and the statistics.

A Law Is a Law Until It Is No Longer a Law

What we are building up to is the fact that the law of gravity is called a "law" because, in billions and billions of observations, not once has any documented event occurred where two objects did not attract each other in precisely the way predicted (we now know that gravity may not work exactly as Newton thought, but like Newton predicted, objects affect distance). We can say with an absolutely incredible degree of statistical certainty that the gravitational "force" between two objects will always affect the distance between them. At this point in time there is probably less than one chance in 1,000,000,000,000 x 10 raised to the 1,000,000,000,000,000th power that gravity will not act essentially as expected. Yet, despite the incredible certainty of gravity, we do not and cannot know whether it is or is not possible for one contrary event to occur, and thus for the law of gravity to be proven wrong!

We are not suggesting the law of gravity is incorrect and that an event whereby it is proven wrong will ever occur. In fact we would be surprised if any of the basic scientific laws of the universe are fundamentally wrong. What we are saying is no matter how many times something has been observed to be true, no matter how incredibly unlikely an unexpected event will occur, we have no way of knowing if such an event is possible or impossible! If the unexpected event is not possible, it will never occur, and it will never be observed. If the event is possible, and if it does occur, then it has happened, period.

We must remember it is not the "law" which makes objects behave in a certain way, fundamental forces far beyond human comprehension do that. Rather the law describes the behavior and remains valid and true only until a single unexpected observation proves it wrong. Actually the law remains only apparently valid and true, if it is later proven wrong its former truth was an illusion. The law was in fact always false.

"Modifying" a theory to better fit observations does not help render the original theory true, rather it creates a new theory that is itself either true or false. Since scientific theories are tested by observation, they are true if and only if each and every event they describe and predict, from the beginning of the universe to the end, in fact occurs exactly as expected. Theories, no matter how solid they might seem, must be discarded as false the very first time they fail to describe real events.

Science is based on observation, formulation of theories, and more observation. To observe necessarily requires the ability to perceive - to sense, feel, smell, touch, taste, see, hear. Early humans used all their senses to explore the world around them. When human senses proved inadequate, they devised better and better tools and instruments to extend their range. Microscopes and telescopes to expand vision, stethoscopes and amplifiers to increase hearing, plus thousands of other sensitive devices to enhance our abilities.

The catalog of devices used to expand our human senses is enormous and growing by the minute, yet all the instruments of humankind can do no more than extend the reach of humans into the universe of which they and their instruments are a part. We know of three spatial dimensions, height, width, depth, and a fourth dimension, time (which may also prove to be spatial in nature). Space (height, width, depth), and "time" all exist together as space-time and cannot exist alone. Is there a fifth, a sixth, a seventh, an eighth dimension? No one knows, for if they exist they appear to be separate and beyond human ability to sense, measure, and thus scientifically prove.

Does that mean those dimensions do not exist, the answer is no. Mathematicians and physicists use formulas to describe sub-atomic phenomena (e.g. - string theory) that can be interpreted as happening in multi-dimensional space. If a fifth dimension exists, it exists. If a fifth dimension does not exist, it does not exist. This is true regardless of whether we can, or never can, observe that dimension and is true for any sixth dimension, seventh dimension, eighth dimension, etc. It is important to realize that no matter how many dimensions are eventually observed, one or more additional dimensions may or may not exist beyond human ability to observe.

Many of you are saying to yourselves it is one thing to say that a dimension beyond human ability to observe may exist, but an entirely different thing to say that one probably does. You are right. Most of you will go on to say it is highly improbable, maybe less than one chance in a trillion, that even one more dimension exists beyond the observable number of dimensions, however many that may eventually prove to be. If you think that, you are wrong. To be able to statistically predict the likelihood of an event happening we must first observe to see how often the event occurs during a given period of time. If we cannot observe the event when it occurs, we cannot determine how often it happens (or conversely, does not happen) and we cannot calculate the likelihood of the event (mathematical models may predict the existence of that which cannot be observed, but they cannot contribute to statistical proof).

One problem with recognizing the limitations of statistical analysis is understanding the difference between not observing an event where the event watched for can be observed, and not observing an event where the event cannot be observed because it is beyond human ability to sense. The first, not observing an event which could be seen, leads to the statistically valid conclusion that the event is unlikely to occur. The second, not observing an event beyond human ability to perceive, an event beyond experimental observation, cannot lead to any conclusion at all about the reality of that event. Yet it appears to be human nature to assume that things which have never been observed do not exist, or at best are highly unlikely to exist.

If something exists beyond human perception it will never be observed during our physical lifetimes. If you cannot measure something because it is beyond human perception you cannot prove it exists, on the other hand you cannot prove that it does not exist! More importantly, you cannot say that it is statistically likely or unlikely that it exists. You simply cannot say anything objective at all about that which is beyond human ability to observe.

It is very, very important to realize that it is absolutely impossible to say that it is either likely or unlikely something exists beyond human observation. We simply cannot determine in any way the probability that something exists, or does not exist, beyond our observable universe. To understand the significance of this often overlooked statement is to understand that we have absolutely no idea what, if anything, lies beyond our cognitive boundaries.

A moment's thought should bring the realization that this absolute limit of statistics and science renders all scientific proof, as well as subjective feelings, that nothing exists beyond our perception into philosophic arguments. Despite what science might claim to have proven, and despite what we might feel, about what lies beyond our ability to observe, we cannot say anything objective about that which is beyond human perception. We may create mathematical models of what should lie somewhere just beyond observation, yet without a means of testing these projections they can never be more than idle speculation. We simply cannot say that it is likely, or not likely, that a world or worlds exist beyond the physical world in which we live. From an analytical standpoint anything, or nothing, may exist beyond human cognition.

Human beings are limited to observing the effects of fundamental forces on matter and energy and must draw conclusions based only on such observations. We can never view the forces themselves, forces whose metaphysical existence and purpose transcend human observation and comprehension. One of the consequences of being only a small part of the universe in which we live is the absolute fact that, unless revealed to us by the whole, we can never know if something or someone exists beyond the limits of our senses. No one, not you nor I nor the smartest person on earth can determine whether or not anything exists beyond that which we can observe.

The significance of the continued possibility that an unexpected event will occur to disprove even the best of theories, and the very fact such a possibility will always exist, renders it impossible to prove anything to be absolutely true or false. Since even the most incredibly supported laws are always subject to being disproved by the happening of a single contrary event, all laws and theorems and common sense proofs are subject to being disproved. Fundamental precepts that apples fall, water flows, fire burns, may all be disproved by future events.

Our limitations not only prevent us from exploring that which is beyond human perception, but also add to all human observations a degree of uncertainty that cannot be overcome. We can never say with total certainty that anything is true, or for that matter, untrue. In this age of science it is hard for those who have not studied the scientific method in detail to understand that, because it is a tool of human beings, it is necessarily limited in its application by the limits of human comprehension and understanding.

It is even harder to accept that, since we are only a part of the whole universe, we can never determine by ourselves what the entire universe is like. A part of something never knows what the whole is like unless the whole makes itself known to the part. We can never know what is true unless the truth is revealed to us. Being a part of the whole means that every law we construct must be built from unprovable assumptions, assumptions that may or may not hold true in the future. We can never know if something, or someone, outside our perception will alter all or part of what we observe, rendering untrue in an instant the very best of our proofs.

Of course, if underlying forces do exist, are not changed, and require the predicted behavior, then the laws never can and never will be disproved. However, that does not alter the fact that it is, and always will be, beyond human ability to prove anything. There is absolutely no way human beings can determine if fundamental forces exist that will never change. We simply cannot determine if it is possible, or if it is not possible, for a contrary event to occur. We can never be certain that contrary events will not happen, we can never prove that anything is absolutely true.

You Can't Believe Your Eyes

We must be sure of observations that are within the bounds of human perception, and skeptical if what we observe appears to be opposite to that which is predicted. Yet we must also be willing to recognize and accept valid experimental data that disproves popular theories. Scientists have declared many theories to be true and elevated them to the status of law, only to discover that future observations, often more accurate than the first, proved them wrong. There are millions of examples of these errors. Perhaps the most famous was the early contention that the earth was flat, a scientific "fact" based on observations that appeared sound to early scholars,\ and which should not be so surprising to those of us who live in hilly country without a visible horizon. What all of us, including scientists, must be aware of is the ease in which we convert our theories into laws. Even if we believe our minds are open most of us grab onto favorite theories and assumptions. We think of, and talk about, them as though there is no doubt they are true.

We should take a minute to discuss the potentially seductive nature of misinterpreted or misused scientific proof. A portion of my high school biology text described the propulsion method of certain one-cell microscopic animals (protozoa) through water by declaring they waved a tail like projection back and forth. The book had been careful to label many new ideas as theories but stated this particular description in absolute terms since these one-celled animals had been observed for many, many years always moving in exactly the same way. Anyone reading the text would believe, as scientists and everyone else did, that there was absolutely no question how the animals got around.

As I was watching television almost ten years later I was surprised to hear of an accidental discovery by a scientist looking at some protozoa. Trying to hold one still under a microscope he held down the tail with a needle. Instead of the body of the animal thrashing back and forth as it should have he observed it to be spinning around the tail. The tail was attached to the body by what was in effect a small rotating joint which acted like an electric motor spinning a propeller. Looking more closely, the scientist discovered the tail was in fact shaped like a corkscrew. Because the microscopic view had always been two dimensional, rather than three, the corkscrew motion looked down on from above had appeared to be that of a wave.

Since it was common to find waving tails in larger animals and since no one had predicted, let alone observed, a 360 degree rotating joint, the thoughts and conclusions of generations of scientists had been colored by conscious and subconscious assumptions. What had been accepted as true turned out to be false. But remember, what was found to be true had in fact always been true.

Similarly, I remember reading an article by a learned scientist who was upset when a well-accepted theory was challenged. He noted that of course it was a theory, just as all scientific laws are really theories, but he then stated that the particular theory was so well documented it was obviously true. It was and is not "obviously true" for, as we have seen, no theory can be said to be unquestionably true.

The theory was the theory of evolution. Darwin's theory has become for many the shining example of humankind's ability to pull itself out of the dark ages, and thus is cloaked in an emotional blanket that associates all criticism of it with attacks on science. To the religious fundamentalist evolution is a tool atheists use to infiltrate the minds of children. To the humanistic scientist evolution is a symbol of the triumph of scientific reasoning over myth. To most people, perhaps, it is simply a more or less correct method of describing the seemingly natural progression of things.

We have little trouble with the idea of either accepting or rejecting evolution, for we can take it or leave it as a part of the physical explanation of the universe which neither conflicts with, nor supports, religion or other science. We would be extremely surprised if the theory of evolution, in some form or another, is not essentially correct. What is troublesome to us is that reasoned challenges to evolution and other theories scientists adopt as scientifically self-evident are often viewed as a return to the irrationality that preceded science. As such they are rejected without consideration as unworthy intrusions into pure science which will go away if ignored.

Many scientists simply will not talk about anything that upsets their idea of reality, yet all theories do just that. When any theory is first proposed it is by its very nature an extension of humankind's knowledge (whether such knowledge is illusory or not) and as such goes beyond the then accepted view of the world. So long as such extensions are orderly and slow there is no problem, but when they leap ahead into the future they become the immediate concern of scientists who wish to keep science "pure". There is a strong presumption that something that has not been proven is somehow less than true. To many people the unproved is not simply unproven, but is fantastic and worthy only of the title science fiction.

Thus, despite professed neutrality on that which has not been confirmed or rejected by experiment many scientists have made it clear they are ready to label as absurd that which is significantly outside common experience and which has not been subjected to empirical scrutiny. If popular theories do not withstand future scientific challenges, recognition of their weakness will be slow to come and acceptance of more exotic alternatives will be resisted with cries that the alternate theories are irrational myths. One should feel uneasy that correct theories which are not subject to easy testing might be dismissed as absurd. If something is currently "unproved" it may well be rejected by scientists as an impossibility, no one beyond the person postulating the theorem may dare dream of its truth.

As we have already noted, in addition to rejecting that which may be proven in the future, many scientists are equally willing to reject as an impossibility the existence of that which is beyond human perception, and thus "unprovable". No matter what we may think, or intuitively "feel", we absolutely cannot reach any objective conclusions about that which is beyond human ability to prove or disprove. We can say nothing objective at all about the "unprovable". The as of yet unproved, as well as the unprovable, may or may not be true.

We should note one type of statement, the definition, which can be viewed as an irrefutable truth. By definition water boils at 100 degrees Celsius. You can always define something to be what you want it to be, yet no matter how you define an event you will not alter the physical reality that makes up the event. Water boils at 100 degrees because we have defined what water does at that temperature to be boiling. The word boiling is nothing more than a word chosen to describe what happens at a given temperature. As a definition it is a label which has nothing to say about the physical laws that affect the water.

While we are as certain as we can be that water will continue to boil at 100 degrees, there can be no absolute guarantee that water will continue to act like it does when it gets to 100 degrees. If in the future the behavior of water changes scientists must either continue to label the new activity as "boiling" by broadening the meaning of the word, or must coin a new word to describe the changed state. If water would solidify instead of vaporizing, scientists could continue to define the new behavior as "boiling" and no one could say they were wrong. Yet the new state would be totally opposite to the old, only the name would remain the same. Fortunately, most observers recognize a responsibility not to use language to define away challenges to their beliefs, therefore they create new words to label new events. The thing to remember is that definitions do not explain or alter the underlying reality.

Reality Is Unreal

We know science cannot tell us anything about the world beyond our perception. What then can it tell us about the reality that surrounds us? Is it able to give us a sturdy foundation on which to build our lives? Can it answer our daily questions? We will explore a bit of modern physics to see just how stable, or unstable, science really is. The information in this section is based on generally accepted theories at the time of writing, please note that by the time you read this book these theories may have been replaced by equally exotic scientific descriptions of reality. No matter what millennium you live in you will be able to discover and recognize the absolute limits of science.

If we are to accept our observations of falling apples as proof of the law of gravity we must first assume several things, for instance, that our eyes accurately perceive the motion of the apple, that our ruler accurately measures the distance the apple travels, and that our watch correctly records the time it takes for it to drop. If confronted with the question "does the ruler you are using shrink and grow if you look at it while moving at different speeds?", most of us would laugh and say to ourselves of course it doesn't, a fixed length is what makes a ruler a ruler. We would think the person asking the question would have us questioning whether the apple is real.

Indeed we would have you question all scientific facts, for a scientist named Einstein shook the assumptions about distance, time, and space that scientists had relied on for thousands of years. In his theory of relativity he proved the length measured on a perfect ruler and the time measured on a perfect clock vary according to the relative motion of one object to another.

Because the change in length and time is unbelievably small where relative speeds are slow, as in the case of a falling apple observed by an earthbound viewer, we can ignore the effect of relativity on everyday life. None-the-less the effects are real and sensitive instruments have confirmed them. Because our eyes cannot measure any change in length does not mean that it is not occurring. The effect on a ruler becomes so great when relative speeds approach the speed of light that what was measured to be a foot would actually become a millionth of a millionth of a millionth of an inch.

Time is also affected by relative motion. If an identical twin could travel to another planet and back in a spaceship that flies at speeds approaching the speed of light, on return to Earth the space traveler would find that they had aged much less than their sibling. Perhaps the astronaut would be only thirty years old while the earthbound twin would be ninety! This is not science fiction, the radical results predicted by relativity have been confirmed by countless experiments, including experiments where atomic clocks placed in jet planes ran slower than their earthbound counterparts!

Here is another example of an everyday fact taken for granted as being absolutely true. What is the shortest distance between two points? Without hesitation the answer for many, many years was a straight line. The theory of relativity tells us the universe may be shaped like a pie-crust with bumps and valleys. Thus, the shortest distance between any two points in the universe, whether it is between towns on earth or stars in space, must be drawn on the surface of the lumpy crust (the area outside the crust is outside the universe and does not exist) and therefore must be slightly curved! The curvature is infinitesimally small, none-the-less the shortest distance between two points may be a slightly curved (geodesic) line!

Over the last few decades, some of the things which have been discovered are that energy and matter are different forms of the same thing (energy = mass times the speed of light squared); the speed of light is constant and nothing can go faster than that speed; as matter approaches the speed of light it becomes infinitely massive and shrinks in its direction of motion to become infinitely small; at the sub-atomic level matter is neither a particle nor a wave but is incomprehensibly both; etc. There are several excellent books written for non-scientists that explain relativity and other topics in modern physics.

Another foundation of modern science, quantum physics, appears to offer a description of reality that is radically different from the one relativity gives us. Rather than giving a single observable solution to a problem, laws that operate at the subatomic quantum level provide probabilities of observing one of many possible results. Quantum mechanics is a relatively new branch of science developed to explain why subatomic particles do not behave according to the Newtonian and relativistic laws that describe the behavior of larger objects. Just prior to the time subatomic particles and events were first measured, physicists had declared that, with very minor exceptions, all the fundamental forces and laws of the universe had been discovered and described. When scientists started to apply the traditional laws of physics to nuclear reactions they were literally amazed to find that the laws did not work! The search was on for a way to modify Newton's and Einstein's laws to explain the new phenomena. At the time no one knew the explanations would shake the very foundations of western knowledge.

Light is made up of energy in the form of photons which have mass (in motion) and which behave like particles, some of the time. The rest of the time photons behave like waves of energy, similar to ocean waves. If you think about an ocean wave you will realize water making up the wave simply moves up and down, not forward. Only the wave itself moves forward. Thus if a boat is sitting a mile from shore, each wave will cause it to rise and fall but will do little to move it toward shore. The boat will move a bit as each successive wave exerts a slight pushing force in the direction of the shore, but the boat won't be carried to shore by any one wave as the wave itself sweeps toward land. The vast majority of the water is simply moving up and down, while only the wave moves forward.

The problem occurs when you try to measure photons using different tests. Some tests detect particles of light hitting targets while other tests detect wave interference when light passes through narrow slits. Back to the ocean example, when two ocean waves meet they either cancel each other if the trough of one overlaps the crest of the other OR they reinforce each other when the crest of one joins the crest of the other, forming a single doubly big wave (any combination in between can occur). When two waves interact they are said to be interfering with each other.

The problem is a particle CANNOT act like a wave and a wave CANNOT act like a particle, yet photons act like both! The solution of modern physics to this apparently unsolvable problem is to say that photons are neither waves nor particles until they are measured and that the measurement itself determines the nature of the photon. In other words, it is the measurement of the event that determines the nature of the event.

To some degree this phenomenon can be said to express hidden problems with what reality really is. In a sense physics is not able to describe the reality of an individual photon since it appears to have two inconsistent, coexistent, yet separate, natures. To the extent the point at which a photon is measured (known as the collapse of the wavefunction) can be considered an event, an unsolved dilemma occurs in determining when the event "actualizes". If light is both a wave and a particle until measured, is it truly a wave (when measured as a wave by an interference experiment) at the point it interferes with itself, or at the point it strikes a photographic plate, or at the time the film is developed, or at the point a human observes the final picture, etc.? The answer is simply not known.

One of the greatest scientific shocks of this century came in the form of the Heisenberg uncertainty principal. As far as many scientists and philosophers were concerned the last straw was when, to help explain the observed phenomena, Heisenberg noted that if you measure the momentum of one of the particles (momentum is velocity, which is speed in a given direction times mass) that make up an atom you must in some way affect its position in an undeterminable way. For example, if you measure the momentum of a subatomic particle by "observing" it move over a given distance, the observation alters its position in some unpredictable manner. Similarly, if you measure position you must alter momentum, thus at any given moment you CAN NEVER measure both the exact momentum and exact position of a subatomic particle.

The more precise you are in measuring momentum the less precise you will be about position, and vice versa. The problem is actually more than a problem of measurement, to be more accurate the wave function of a subatomic particle (which describes the particle at the quantum level) that has not been observed is precisely determined (without using probabilities) by a formula known as Schrodinger's wave equation. However, the very moment you attempt to measure the momentum or position of the particle, the wave function collapses introducing probabilities into the equation, and the exact momentum and position of the particle CANNOT be determined.

Heisenberg's theory can be interpreted as supporting the proposition that at the quantum level the very concepts of momentum and position have no real meaning. At the level of measured observation modern physics can tell you how many particles in a group of particles have certain momentums and positions, and how many have other momentums and positions, but physicists CANNOT tell you what the momentum and position of any one particle is. This failure is far more than just some inability to measure momentum and position, it is due to the fact that it is fundamentally uncertain what the momentum and position of any single observed particle is! A single particle when measured simply does not have position and momentum in any normal sense of the words, but members of a group do, and the probability of x number having x momentum and x, y, z position can be precisely computed!

One interpretation (there are others) of this finding is that nature appears to determine the behavior of its particles by a flip of a coin. Einstein spent the latter part of his life attempting to disprove this disturbing idea, it flew against his concept of the universe and prompted him to say "My God does not throw dice". Yet he was unable to disprove quantum theory in general, and the included uncertainty principal in particular, both of which have correctly predicted every subatomic event that they have been tested against!

To emphasize the significance of the uncertainty principal remember it says that the uncertainty about momentum and position is not due to limitations on humankind's ability to make measurements, but rather is based on the apparent fact that when observed the momentum and position of an individual particle is fundamentally uncertain. Of course, future physicists may find an underlying set of rules that can be used to predict the behavior of individual particles, or may discover a fundamental unified law which is consistent with the observed behavior (an atemporal model may be found that works). Einstein's discomfort may well have been the result of human limitations on his understanding of God. Even though many questions remain unanswered, repudiation of the uncertainty principal, however comforting it would be to philosophers, seems uncertain at best.

One current theory, which we mentioned earlier, that is popular among cosmologists and that would eliminate the uncertainty, shows just how confusing and exotic the universe may be. The truly wild (and from some scientists' points of view virtually unbelievable) "many-worlds theory", suggests that every time an event occurs which has a possible required alternative, the universe splits into two identical parts, except that in one universe one alternative occurs, while in the other the other alternative occurs. As we discussed earlier, according to this theory (or at least to the most popular interpretations of it) there are potentially an infinite number of identical, except for the required alternatives, versions of each of us living simultaneously in different worlds. Uncertainty is eliminated because every alternative is guaranteed to occur. Rather than being a model of reality this idea may be a product of human limitations.

If you want some more disturbing news we can give it to you. Quantum physics is faced with the problem of locality. For example, components of atoms have a property called spin. Spin is one of the fundamental quantities in the universe that must, and we do mean must, be conserved. For each particle that possesses positive spin, there MUST exist a particle with negative spin.

Two entangled particles with opposite spin can fly off in different directions from an atom. So far, no problems. We can change the spin of one of the entangled particles. The very instant we do so the other particle's spin changes, no matter what the distance is that separates them! Physicists are at a loss to explain how a particle in a different location without any means of communication knows what another particle's spin is. It is a mystery how one particle knows to change spin at the very instant the spin of the other particle is altered (many experiments seem to confirm the phenomena).

Einstein believed that any "rational", in the sense of "objective", description of nature is incomplete unless it is both a local and realistic theory. A theory is realistic if a particle has intrinsic properties that exist even before they are measured. A theory is local if measuring the properties of one particle cannot affect the properties of another, physically separated particle, in a length of time that would require communication between the particles that is faster than the speed of light. Yet quantum entanglement of spatially separated particles appears to require that realism, or locality, or both, be violated!

One speculative explanation of entanglement eliminates the normal assumption of locality, the assumption that events occur at one specific location in the space-time continuum. If it is possible to have a rational description of the universe without a local theory, then you can have events that appear to be occurring in different locations actually occurring in the same place. Thus, no matter how far apart they may seem to be, two particles could know each other's spin because they are, in some as yet unexplained manner, in the same location. Perhaps the two particles occupy the same position in some unknown dimension where there is no such thing as separation. Perhaps events in our universe are relative in a deeper sense than we realize, and our universe is both atemporal and aspatial. Speculation about the significance of lack of locality is really unproductive, except to note that lack of locality could help explain premonitions and extrasensory events.

No matter what the current scientific view is toward non-local events, evidence that quantum entanglement is real strongly suggests some kind of instantaneous communication between particles, or some other unknown, more exotic explanation. The only known rational explanation for the instantaneous change of state of two particles separated by extraordinary distances is that information about the state of one particle travels to the other particle without the passage of time. If this is in fact what happens, it would appear to offer support for our difficult conclusions.

Other complex examples of conflicts with accepted concepts of reality, truth, and classical philosophy and logic, are found within the fascinating, unsettling, discoveries of modern physics. We are left with fundamental paradoxes, the solutions to which are totally unknown. Indeed, despite what we are told by many scientists, it is not at all clear to those working at the leading edge of scientific inquiry that an objective physical description of the universe actually exists. The destruction of traditional concepts of time, space, matter, energy, of life itself, is both frightening, and hopeful.

Given the dramatic efforts of modern physics to unravel the mysteries of the physical world, coupled with the possibility of the discovery of theories that better explain space-time (or atemporal space), perhaps even the discovery and/or existence of other dimensions, all manner of extraordinary event may eventually be explained. Yet it is also possible that, despite appearances to the contrary, the universe does not have an objective and/or observable fundamental physical nature, and that no explanation is possible.

Again we need to remember that all theories owe their credibility to repeated statistical successes. Even in the case of generally accepted physical laws, like the ones we have just discussed, one observed deviation would result in the probability of the theorem being correct going to zero. When a theory is for the first time shown to be false it is not merely more likely to be false, IT IS FALSE. On the other hand, the more observations reported which confirm the predictions of a law, the higher the probability is that the law is true. No matter how many observations are made, the possibility will always exist that the law is in fact false.

Spilled Milk

A brief comment on the creation of the universe and the laws themselves. At the time this book was written it was generally accepted that all of space-time was created at or near a point in time popularly known as the big bang. By the time you read this, science may have discovered a better description for the beginning second of the cosmos, but the possible implications of current knowledge are too interesting not to mention. Entropy is a measure of disorder. If a glass of milk turns over the milk will pour out onto the table, yet one will never see milk flow from a table back into the glass. This is because the entropy (disorder) of the system tends to increase over time. Another example, you may pour cream into your coffee to lighten it, but the cream will never remove itself to make the coffee black again. As a rule, complex systems tend to become more disordered over time.

The universe we live in is a place of amazingly low entropy, were it not so we would not be alive. Each of us is an example of a highly ordered, low entropy system. Every star, planet, rock, tree, living creature, everything in the universe that is more ordered than the diffuse interstellar gas clouds that surround us, is an example of a system with varying degrees of low entropy. Roger Penrose, a noted British mathematician who along with Stephen Hawking established how singularities form in black holes, concludes that: "There is a certain sense in which I would say the universe has a purpose. It's not there just somehow by chance. Some people take the view that the universe is simply there and it runs along... and we happen by accident to find ourselves in this thing. I don't think that's a very fruitful or helpful way of looking at the universe, I think that there is something much deeper about it, about its existence, which we have very little inkling of at the moment."

To be more exact, in his book "The Emperor's New Mind" (Oxford Univ. Press, 1989), Penrose calculated that for our universe to have the extremely low entropy it now has required as the "starting point" at the big bang the selection of a virtually infinitesimally tiny volume of the total phase space of all possible universes (phase space is a complete mathematical description of any physical system). To be more exact, the universe we live in apparently began at a point constituting approximately 1 part in 10 raised to the 10th power raised to the 123rd power ($10^{10^{123}}$) of the entire phase space volume of all possible universes!

As Penrose pointed out, this is a deceptively large number, which in fact cannot be written out! If you tried to write it down by writing the number "1" on a piece of paper, you would have to write a 0 on every single atom in the universe just to approach the number of zeros that follow the one, even then you would not be close to writing out the entire number. This amazing requirement for the initial condition at creation suggests that the odds are no better than 1 in $10^{10^{123}}$ power that the universe in which we live was created by random chance. If the math holds true (visit www.ws5.com/Penrose for the details), and this interpretation is as logical as it seems, it may mean that the chance that the universe was created at random is about as close to impossible as one can get!

Many find comfort in believing that even if science has not yet discovered all of the laws every physical event from creation onward evolved according to a set of absolute physical laws. The mathematically precise physical structure of the universe, the tiny place we have in the incredible vastness of space, the biologic characteristics we share with animals, etc., all may be interpreted as evidence of a purely mechanistic process that governs our lives. Indeed, there is ongoing research trying to explain biophysical evolution in terms of self-ordering / self-replication, perhaps driven by the need to dissipate accumulated energy (e.g. sunlight on the primordial swamp).

Some scientists point to the fact that the odds against spontaneous creation of life from molecules appear to not be exceptionally high. However they are comparing apples and oranges, it is the odds of the random creation of a universe in which spontaneous creation of life could occur that Penrose calculated as being infinitesimally small, not the odds of spontaneous creation of living organisms in that universe after it has been created. Researchers may or may not eventually be able to offer insight into chemistry that could have allowed transition from inanimate molecules to living cells. Even if scientists are successful in proposing a robust mechanism, the statistical impossibility of our low entropy universe being selected from all possible universes remains unchanged.

If we focus on the most fundamental levels we are confronted by the fact that for self-ordering to be possible in the first place there must have been a break in the symmetry of particles and anti-particles, something that has never been observed, otherwise there would have been nothing to organize. If we consider the complexity of that which we observe, the initial extraordinarily low entropy of our universe, matter which should not have survived antimatter, and the mystery of consciousness, and if we are honest with ourselves, we cannot escape the intuitive feeling that there is an "order" in the chaos that cannot be explained by science.

Even if the odds against the random selection of our low entropy universe out of all possible universes are not quite as impossible as they seem, we simply cannot ignore the intuitive feeling that the odds are almost infinitely against the random creation and existence of everything around us. Think about this for a while. No matter how strongly we may feel that life is the result of physical processes only, if we are objective we must admit that it intuitively seems impossible that a random physical process could create the almost infinitely complex, yet extremely well ordered, low entropy universe in which we live.

While it seems that the underlying laws of the universe could not have been created by chance, we have no explanation why it also often appears that the observable physical universe deterministically evolves according to complex statistical laws. We don't know why reality is such that life appears to many as nothing more than a complex, biologic process, riddled with physical imperfections. We are not willing to say that the universe does not appear to exhibit many of the characteristics of a physical entity devoid of the non-physical.

None-the-less, there is no objective statistical support for the conclusion that the world in which we live is the result of purely physical processes. No matter how hard we might try to ignore them, we are confronted by astronomical odds against random selection of a set of initial conditions that could create a low entropy universe that exhibits the complexity of our universe. Anyone who takes the time to try to visualize billions of stars bursting out of a pinhead is faced with a mystery which, if we are honest with ourselves, leaves us at the very least with the possibility, however slight we may believe it to be, that the observable physical universe is not "all there is".

It is very, very, important to understand that no matter what you may have been told or what you may think, no human being has any idea whatsoever what the fundamental physical nature of the universe really is. The consensus is that our universe began as a single, almost infinitely massive, almost infinitely small, speck. As of this date, no one has been able to comprehend, let alone explain, the mechanism during the microsecond of the Planck epoch that allowed the universe to expand from a dot smaller than an atom, into the billions upon billions of stars that fill our universe.

Anyone who takes the time to try to visualize this process will realize the impossibility of making sense of what appears to be a scientific fact. No one has a clue how to understand the reality of a quantum particle that is quite literally everywhere at the same time. No one knows how the action at a distance that relativity suggests cannot occur, actually does occur, if it really does. No one knows how to define or quantify human consciousness. There is only one scientific deduction we can be certain of, and that is that human beings do not know and understand the fundamental nature of physical reality.

What all this tells us is that we have no real idea at all what the true nature of our life on earth is or what the possibilities are for our continued existence after death! We are so much a part of the tiny portion of universe in which we live that we seldom realize the significance of our limitations. Instead of viewing our lack of knowledge as profound and exciting we tend to accept with curious apathy that there may be far more to our existence than we know.

At this point in our journey we are not trying to suggest that anything exists beyond our perceived universe, nor are we trying to suggest that nothing exists beyond our known universe. We are not suggesting if we survive the grave we will find ourselves in some dimension beyond the one we can sense and measure during our physical lives, perhaps so, perhaps not. Nor are we saying that we can or cannot sense and know about that which lies beyond the grave, if anything, until we experience physical death.

What we are saying is scientific study and statistical analysis are absolutely limited to that which we can observe and measure. The absence of scientific proof does not make it less likely, nor make it more likely, that something which is true and real lies beyond human observation. The important thing to remember is that no matter how likely or unlikely you "FEEL" it is that something exists, if it is beyond human ability to observe, you CANNOT "KNOW" if it is likely or unlikely that it does exist.

This is true for the probability of the existence of life after death. From a scientific standpoint we simply cannot say it is likely that life after death exists. It is equally true that we absolutely cannot say it is likely that life after death does not exist. While scientists may offer attributes of physical death as proof that human beings do not exist beyond the grave the real answer to the question lies beyond human ability to scientifically prove, one way or the other. Indeed, we cannot say anything objective at all about the possibility of life after death. If life after death does not exist, it does not exist, period. If life after death does exist, it does exist, period.

Many of you will read what we have just discussed, agree with it, and then let it fade out of your mind as you move on to whatever comes next. If what we are saying is true it is fundamental and "profound". Perhaps it will be important and helpful to you later on when we discuss what may be the most important choice in your life. For this reason we urge you to think carefully about what has been said so that you will understand what we are talking about.

Why?

Before leaving our discussion of the scientific method, we should note the interesting, apparently absolute, limit whereby the question "how" becomes the question "why". Let's jump ahead 10,000 years and assume that a unified field theory has been discovered. A unified field theory is a theory which describes the behavior of all forces and elements according to a set of fairly simple laws. If and when such a theory is proved we may in fact have succeeded in explaining the past, present, and future behavior of all observed matter and energy. However, the ultimate questions will remain. Why were the unified forces that control energy and matter created? If there was no creation, if the forces always existed, why did they always exist? Why do any forces exist? Who or what is the source of such primordial forces if they are the most fundamental of forces? These will still be unanswered, and it is not hard to see, will remain unanswerable.

Science will have succeeded in fully describing the forces seen in nature and their effects on matter and energy. The question how forces work will, for the most part, have been answered. But an explanation of the creation, the existence, the source of the forces, the answer to why such forces exist, will be missing. The ultimate question WHY? clearly defines the limits of science and human beings.

Without realizing it, we constantly bump against this invisible wall that surrounds us and limits our knowledge. We know that the force of gravity causes objects to be attracted to each other, but why is this so? Think about it for a few minutes. Obviously gravity needs to exist to prevent objects from flying apart, but why not have a gravity that is half as strong, or maybe two times stronger? At a more fundamental level, why does it matter if objects fly apart or stay together? Why do sub-atomic particles group together to form atoms that form molecules that eventually form us? Why do matter and energy even exist? We can reason that laws act like they do to preserve the order of the universe, but that answer really begs the question why the universe has any order in the first place?

In this increasingly scientific era many of us have lost the wonder we once had when we looked at the physical world. For example, we take for granted the widely accepted fact that all that is in the universe started as an almost infinitesimally small speck of energy/matter. Because science tells us how the universe evolved from a tiny fraction of a second after the big bang up to today, we assume that science can tell us why that initial speck exponentially exploded into that which surrounds us. Yet science cannot explain the ultimate origin and existence of what we euphemistically call physical reality.

Despite all that we have discovered, despite what future insights the scientific method may yield, science cannot deduce the physical origin of the universe. Each of us should recognize, and be continually amazed by, the infinite complexity of the reality that surrounds us which appears to have evolved from infinite simplicity. We should live in a state of wonder at the fact that the question why is a profound mystery beyond the ability of science and humankind to answer.

Furthermore, the question why imposes subtle limits on our ability to fully answer the question how. Future scientists may build what appears to be a unified model of how things work, yet the impossibility of scientifically discovering why the universe is as it is also affects our ability to fully understand how it works. Just as we cannot say why the initial conditions of the universe were as they were, we cannot construct an objective model of the universe that tells us with absolute certainty how those initial conditions evolved from essentially nothing.

This is more than saying that nothing existed before the initial conditions, rather it is based on the apparent fact that initial conditions are the most basic elements of physical existence. Even if the universe had no beginning, if the initial conditions did not evolve but rather simply existed, we cannot build an objective physical model that explains the fundamental nature of an initial condition. Because we can never answer the ultimate question why, we cannot fully understand the initial conditions and therefore can never answer with absolute certainty the ultimate questions why and how the initial conditions evolved.

We should note in passing that the anthropic principle points out that if the laws of the universe were not suitable for our present existence on earth we would simply not be here to ask the question why? Yet applying that principle to the question "why are the laws like they are" invites a less than satisfactory, circular, answer. If we are here because the laws are as they are that does not lead to the logical conclusion that the laws are as they are because we are here, so we are left without an answer to our basic question.

The anthropic answer, along with every other reasonable answer one can give to what we might call an intermediate version of the question why, allows us to continue to ask the ultimate question why? In response to the answer that the laws of the universe are as they are because they must be so for us to be here, the very real question may still be asked, why are we here? Perhaps the only answer we can give to the question "why do forces exist and behave as they do" is "just because" they do. Perhaps, however, the answer is that they behave the way they were designed to behave.

The more we learn, the more humble science becomes. What seemed obvious, now seems vague. If humankind cannot know anything with complete certainty, then science is not the solid rock it appears to be. Scientific discoveries possess an ephemeral quality seldom recognized by observers. Since science has not, and perhaps cannot, discover fundamental laws that guide the physical universe, the failure of modern theories may be the precursor to incredible discoveries which challenge concepts of space and time, uncertainty and determinism, entropy and order, etc. As science matures, the idea that (for want of a better description of the unknown) meaningful additional dimensions may exist seems to be an increasingly comfortable one. No matter what the future of science brings, it is a logical, absolute fact that unless the answer is somehow revealed to us, the ultimate question will remain, WHY?

Truth, Belief, and Faith

We have discussed the fact that we can never be certain anything is true. We have noted that since human knowledge is finite, all attempts at proving things must start with unprovable assumptions. We have considered the limitations on human understanding which make all human assertions of fact simply statements of belief. Does all this mean what we believe to be true but cannot prove is any less true? Again, the answer is no. If something is true it is true whether or not you prove, believe in, or have even thought about, its truth.

Literally billions of ideas and beliefs can be suggested to be true. We can propose assumptions and make eloquent arguments based on those assumptions which will send us off in any direction we might wish to go. Every day we see people who are certain of the absolute truth of their beliefs never realizing they have subconsciously talked themselves into accepting as fundamentally and absolutely true that which is, and must be, based on their assumptions.

Thus, we can argue persuasively that we are descendants of Martians, that inanimate objects talk to each other, that we really do not exist at all, etc., etc., etc. Since we cannot know whether or not something or someone exists beyond our perception, we cannot know if the wildest of ideas may in fact be true somewhere outside our current existence. Yet even though anything may be true, we should not allow ourselves to become casual observers applying logical arguments to first prove and then disprove fundamental beliefs about the nature and meaning of life. What we want to emphasize is that the reader should put aside all assumptions and beliefs; take a journey into their heart, mind, and soul; and then decide what they want to believe is true.

What is true is true. What then is the difference in believing something to be true and proving something is true if indeed the belief is true? The difference is not in the truth of the matter, for what we believe to be true is either true or not regardless of our belief as to its truth. Rather the difference lies in the realization that what appears absolutely true may not be true.

If we cannot prove anything how do we determine what is true? If the best we can do is believe something is true what good is that? The answer lies in what we just said, if what we believe to be true is true then not being able to prove it is true is not important.

We have been talking as though we start with the belief that everything we seek to prove is untrue and then go from there. The fact is that we have built into our existence a set of assumptions that certain things are true, assumptions that we base our strongest beliefs on. For example, though nothing can be proven beyond doubt few would argue the world they live in does not actually exist, or a ball thrown into the air will not fall back to earth, or people do not grow older. Few doubt or question the solid reality of any of the events that make up everyday life, from the esoteric proposition the sun will rise to the reality of mundane chores associated with living.

All you are, all you have been, everything about your life contributes to your belief in the truth of millions upon millions of things. Your life, and your perception of it, is an incredibly intricate web of observations, feelings, and experiences, all parts of your existence, all making you, you. Perhaps humans have some inexplicable intuition that gives them insight into what is actually true, perhaps not. The fact is that all anyone can do is to use all the abilities they have to determine what is true. All you can do is to do what you can to think, and analyze, and test, and rethink, until you believe something is true.

In many cases the scientific method appears to serve us well when we search for the "truth". This is particularly so when we sort through results of objective tests to analyze which drug is most effective or what car is best. In other cases logic proves inadequate and feelings seem a better guide. Philosophy and religion are both ill-suited to scientific inquiry. Because they deal with that which is beyond human perception philosophical and religious beliefs must come from within each individual and must be based on all that makes an individual a unique human being. Such beliefs grow when experiences of life combine with that illusive quality that makes each of us the singular person we are.

How much, if any, of the process of determining such fundamental belief is guided by insight, and how much is a product of heredity and environment, is a question without answer. We have seen many people paralyzed by the fear that what they believed to be true might be false. Over the years we have come to believe that if anyone puts a sincere effort into determining what is true, and perhaps what is good, they will succeed. Even though they will never be able to prove anything, what they find themselves believing to be true and good will be, perhaps

76

even if not perfectly correct, what actually is true and good. There is, of course, no proof for such a belief, yet it is one of our strongest intuitive beliefs.

We are not suggesting that someone who has determined his or her answer to a question before searching for it will ever find the true answer. Those who want to prove their point, even if it is only to themselves, will inevitably mold everything to fit their answer. With varying degrees of discomfort, they will reach their previous conclusion every time.

What we are saying is that we are convinced that those who search their hearts, minds, and souls to understand life will find themselves believing certain things to be true and right. Perhaps these more or less inherent beliefs are simply products of human existence and thought. Perhaps, however, they are insights into profound fundamental truths.

What about the times when you feel strongly that something is or might be true, but are uncertain of those feelings because, to some degree, your beliefs lie outside human perception or experience? Beyond mere belief is something called faith. When our beliefs are strong we may choose to have faith in their truth. What then is faith?

In part faith is having an intense conviction what you believe to be true is in fact true, but it is more than that. Real faith in the truth of something is a product of your total being. It is not only what you believe to be true, but what you want to be true. Faith is a total commitment by you to believe that what you think should be true is true, that what you think should be right and good is in fact right and good.

Those who have faith vary in their intensity of belief. Some are so convinced of the goodness of what they have faith in that, no matter what happens to cast doubt on their beliefs, they are determined to hold onto their faith for as long as they live. For them there is no alternative, they have faith that what they believe to be true is, if truth exists at all, true. Others have a faith that may be weakened by the conflicting beliefs of friends or by the influence of unexpected events.

You cannot have faith in something or someone simply because there is nothing better to believe in. Faith cannot be based on negative choices but must be based on a real, strong, sometimes total, desire that what you believe should be true actually is true. You must want what you have faith in to be true. Since nothing can be fully proved or disproved, unless truth has been somehow revealed, that which people have faith in is, for them, that which is true.

The End May be Just the Beginning

What is worth having faith in? Earlier we said if your existence ends with the death of your body it is virtually inconceivable to us that life has any meaning at all. We may be wrong, there may be existential meaning in physical life without life after death. As we have said, those who refuse to believe in life after death must continue to search for existential meaning in this life in which to believe. None-the-less, we believe that your existence has meaning only if you continue to exist in some form or fashion after the death of your body. It seems imperative to us that if there is to be any reason and purpose to your life you must prove or believe or have faith in an existence beyond the grave.

Again, just because we cannot prove something is true does not in any way mean it is not true. Because we cannot prove, or disprove, we continue to exist after the death of our bodies does not mean that we do not continue to exist, or that we do. If we continue to exist after our physical death, then we continue to exist, and if we do not, then we do not.

In support of our conclusions we have the objective fact that the odds that our physical universe was created at random appear to be almost infinitesimally small, and the objective observation that human beings logically and intuitively believe there must be a reason that the infinitely complex universe exists. It is almost impossible for us to believe that the infinitely complex mechanisms of physics from relativity to quantum mechanics, and of biology from DNA to protein folding, all of which are essential to life, have no "meaning". Since it looks like no one can objectively prove they continue to exist after physical death, the question is whether or not you choose to believe you do. Yet existence beyond the grave lies so far beyond human perception and observation, beyond human comprehension and understanding, that human feelings about such existence are inadequate to base substantial beliefs on.

Then is this a matter you should have faith in? Your answer to that question, if it is to be more than a casual one which will not last, must be based on what you believe life is all about, not only after death but also right now. If you are to have faith in a life after death you need to believe people are more than biologic creatures. To be worth having faith in, to be worth wanting, life beyond the grave must be more than just existing through time. It must offer a hope of something worth living for, of goodness, perhaps of joy.

We may imagine many different things about life beyond the grave. We may believe in a metaphysical extension of life, somehow self-perpetuating and dependent only on a communion of some sort of mental energy unique to human beings. We may believe in reincarnation whereby forms change but human beings never die. There is no limit to what we may believe life after death will be like. As we have said, no one can prove us wrong, or right.

Speculation about the "physical" nature of life after death can be little more than guesses and offers little help in making a decision whether or not we would want to live in such a world. If we are more than our physical selves it would seem that there must be more to look forward to in a life after death than the "physical" aspects of that life. We need to find out if there is something beyond the physical that every human must do if they want to be more than worthless travelers in time.

While we cannot say that it is objectively likely or unlikely, if you continue to exist after physical death does it not seem intuitively likely you will retain the intellect and capacity for rational thought we have postulated is essential to your uniqueness? The intuitive answer is that it is indeed likely rational intellectual thought will exist in a world beyond the physical. It seems if you are to remain you, the unique intellect which is a fundamental part of your existence in your present life would continue to exist in the next. Furthermore, it seems intuitively likely that rational thought beyond the constraints of earthly boundaries would be of a much greater character.

If we survive the grave does it not seem intuitively likely that the most positive aspects of our life on earth will also be positive features of the world after death? In looking for a reason to believe in an extension of life beyond the grave that is worth living for, and thus worth having faith in, you must look at this world and this life. Life on earth is the only basis we have on which to project what a world beyond the grave might be like. You must find the most positive aspects of this life, you must find in this life a reason to believe life has meaning and purpose.

Perhaps you will find "good" in this life that gives you a reason to believe, or have faith, that there is a life after death filled with "joy". To help you choose what to believe about life, now and beyond the grave, we need to explore our present lives. We need to consider not only the physical, but also the non-physical aspects of our present existence.

If and when you understand life and know what your life could be like both now and after death, you will be able to choose whether or not you want to have faith that there is something worth living for now and after death. You may choose to have faith that your life has meaning and purpose. You may find that you want to have faith your life will not end at the grave. You may choose to live the kind of life now you hope you will live after death. In the rest of this book, we will be considering whether there is "good" in this life that makes it worth having faith in a life after death.

If we do continue to exist after our physical deaths, then each moment of our lives, both before and after death, may have meaning and purpose. If we survive death then each of us has been, is, and will continue to be a unique being. What then is the meaning and purpose of life? What should, or must, you do? What choices do you have right now?

Many philosophers, psychiatrists, and others argue persuasively that self-satisfaction is the most important human goal. A society made up of individuals who maximize their own well-being is a society at its best. They conclude that when each of us reaches our own point of maximum pleasure all of us benefit. What constitutes the maximization of pleasure is a hotly debated question answered in countless, totally different ways. Ideas range from doing anything that makes you feel "good" to espousing intense dedication to such diverse things as political causes, meditation, or simply the pursuit of pleasure.

Many suggest the free market works well in selecting what is worthwhile in life with various methods of providing pleasure coming and going as demand identifies, supplies, and satisfies needs. Others argue the best society is made up of family groups that seek to maximize the family's happiness. Some extend the group to include friends and even strangers, but often exclude those outside the group's geographic and social spheres. Volume after volume after volume has been written describing what various people believe life is all about. Multitudes of people have dedicated large parts of their lives to convincing others of the truth of their ideas and the wisdom of following their examples.

Instead of closely examining and eliminating one at a time what we believe to be the fallacies and follies of humankind we will suggest to you what many believe life is all about. If you choose to know and understand what is said, we believe you will discover what is true and gives meaning and purpose to life. We are about to look for something in life worth living for, something to have faith in.

What many suggest is worth living for is love. Not what we often call love, but that which is the most profound of human experiences.

Love

The love we are talking about is far more, incredibly more, than that which we normally call love. Love is the most positive of human experiences. It is the deepest, most profound, of human relationships. It is the giving of all you have to give to someone else.

What is love? Love is beyond definition, it cannot be described in words. No effort to describe love can in any way answer what love is. Love is beyond human ability to analyze and evaluate. Yet each of us has, as a part of our very being, an understanding of love. The love we are talking about is basic, profound, a fundamental part of our existence. In each and every one of our hearts and minds, and we believe souls, we know and understand what love is.

Love is so deeply a part of human beings, so far beyond definition and description, so elusive to those who halfheartedly seek it, that you will know and understand love only if you engage in a very personal search of heart and mind and soul which leads to the very essence of your being. To understand life it is necessary to understand love. No one can make you understand love, you alone must be willing to take the inward journey. We will repeatedly urge you to do so, for nothing can take the place of that understanding.

Most of us think we already know what love is, when in fact few do. Sometime during our lives the majority of us will believe we have found true love, even though we have not. Many of us will go to our graves believing we have loved, when we never loved at all.

For most people, their understanding of love is hidden deep within. Each time they glimpse love and feel it trying to surface they push it back to its resting place. Few are willing to search for the love that may be found inside them, few are willing to let their knowledge of love surface. We believe each and every person who truly wants to know and understand love, and who is willing to search and search and search their heart, mind, and soul, will know and understand love.

The search is difficult, it is perhaps the most difficult task you will ever face. If you search your heart, mind, and soul you will find yourself surrounded by multitudes of conflicting feelings, questions, doubts, etc. These will draw your attention away from your search, and may make it seem futile and worthless. If you try to deal with each distraction as it appears you will end up floundering from side to side, without direction, your goal appearing on the horizon yet never getting closer.

Before answering the many questions love poses, before satisfying your doubts, you should complete your search. Search your heart, mind, and soul, your being, to know and understand love. Set aside all questions, doubts, and fears, put all your energy and thought into your search. First understand love, then ask and answer questions about it.

It is very hard to stay on track. Your search will take you through and among daily experiences and deep memories filled with the emptiness, cruelty, and physical pleasures of a world where love is seldom seen. The cold glance of strangers on the street, the reality of poverty in the shadow of enormous wealth, watching people get sick and die a seemingly final death. "Human nature" will try to dictate to you what to think and what to do. Thoughts of food, drink, luxury, sex, all the physical pleasures you could be enjoying pull at your attention and cause your mind to drift. Your focus is blurred as first one thing and then another interrupts your search.

Even when you think you have broken through the fog and are running toward your goal, a tiny diversion, a moment's pause, and you are flung back into that strange and cloudy state of doubts not knowing where, if anywhere, you are. Back in the haze, you may find yourself believing you reached your goal when you did not. This feeling of success can be strong, and the rush of living may make it seem even more real since little time is available to stop and think about who you are, where you have been, and where you are going.

What can happen is that you can make yourself believe you understand love when in fact all you have seen is false illusions of love. You may wrongly conclude that love is really not that special at all. To allow yourself to stop short of your goal, to allow yourself to believe you understand love when you do not, is to condemn yourself to the deep darkness shared by all who live without love. A darkness few recognize, a blackness the depth of which can be appreciated only by those who find love. Only those who finish their search will know and understand love.

Completing the search requires a willingness to start. It is far easier to live your life following whatever sort of daily routine you have, over the years, consciously and subconsciously constructed for yourself, a routine designed to make you feel good about your life. For most of us this means mixing just enough "good" deeds with our daily activities that bring us self-satisfaction and physical pleasure to give us the illusory feeling that we are "good" people. For better or worse you nurture an image of yourself you have been developing since childhood. An image that dictates what is expected of you and rules how you act, making your life a repeating cycle of yesterdays.

Even if you do not feel good about your life you are usually more comfortable not straying too far from the familiar. It is easier to live the "normal" life you have made for yourself than it is to question and search and change. Yet if you want to know and understand love you must give the search your all, without fear of, or resistance to, the changes it may bring in your life. You need to search and search until you know what it means to love, what it would be like to live in a world where each and every person loves every other person.

This is more than a mental exercise. If after your search you believe love is what all people should give each other then you have perhaps not only found what gives life meaning and purpose right now, but also found that which makes it worth having faith in life beyond the grave. At this point we are not suggesting that you embrace without question the ideas of eternity and the goodness of love. We are saying you will find it virtually, or perhaps totally, impossible to decide whether or not to believe that love is worth living for if you do not know and understand what love is. Only when you are willing to search your heart, mind, soul, your very being to know love will you understand the decision to love or not to love. Only then can you make your choice.

In the remaining pages of this book we will give some examples of love, discuss what those who love do, and talk in general about love. Yet nothing we say will bring you an understanding of love, only your search can do that. Your search will begin whenever you want it to, and will end whenever you want it to. This book is useful only if you take the hours, days, months, or years, whatever it takes, to complete your search. If you stop when you find that half-hearted, fleeting, shallow thing most people call "love" your efforts will have been futile and worthless. You will have failed to find what love really is.

It is very easy to stop short of understanding love. The idea of pure, real love is so alien to our experiences, so foreign to the world we live in, we subconsciously, and even consciously, reject it as a non-existent fantasy. Yet it does exist. Because we seldom, if ever, witness such love does not mean it is less than real.

Because the experiences of our past and the realities of our daily existence attack love does not mean it is a fantasy. We may never choose to fill our world with pure love. Yet because each of us can choose love, such a world is possible. Our doubts and fears, desires and temptations, weaknesses and longing to "live", cannot change the fact that pure, true, real, love exists, and that people can love one another.

What Do Those Who Love Do?

If you love someone who is hungry, you will give them food; someone who is thirsty, you will give them water; someone who is cold, you will give them your coat. If you love someone who is sick, you will care for them until they are well; someone who is in prison, you will visit them; someone without a home, you will take them home with you. These are all acts and deeds those who love do for the people they love. Yet love is far more than the doing of any particular act or deed.

While those who love people will do the things we just mentioned simply doing "good deeds" is not the same as loving. Many who do not love do "good deeds". Many who say they love, and perhaps even believe they love, if they love at all do so only halfheartedly and from moment to moment.

It is hard to say that someone who feeds a person when they are hungry and then leaves them to find their own shelter really loves that person. It is hard to call love the giving of money to an orphanage when children's cries for attention and companionship go unanswered. It is difficult to understand how someone can say they love a person when they make that person feel they need to applaud their donor for every gift they receive.

Love is far more than acts, deeds, words, or feelings. To love someone, really love someone, is to give them all you have to give, true, deep, pure, indefinable, indescribable love. It is giving to others the love that you will find and understand if you complete your search of heart, mind, and soul. What we are talking about is love, true, pure, real, love.

If you love, you will help a stranger who needs help, even if it puts you in danger. If you love, you will think first about the needs of those you love, and only then think about your own needs. If you love, you will do what you can, all you can, for everyone you meet. Those who really understand love know in their heart, mind, and soul that love is the greatest thing in life one human being can give another.

If you truly love someone you are giving them your very best. We have reached an awkward point in trying to use language to describe a state of being which affects the totality of human existence. How can we adequately describe how a person who truly loves thinks, feels, and acts? We can't.

Only you can search within yourself to know and understand love. Unless you have completed your search of your heart, mind, and soul and know and understand love, you will not understand what we are saying or what anyone else is saying when they tell you about the love they find in their heart, mind, and soul. So how can you understand what we are saying when we say love is the best part of human life?

As we said, regardless of human inability to describe love we can look inward to know and understand love. And when each of us complete our search and know and understand love we know and understand that love is indeed the most positive element of human existence. We know that the very best each of us can do is to love. We may find it difficult to talk about love with someone who has not yet finished their search, however once a person understands love they join all others who have completed their search in a communion of knowledge which makes communication of ideas about love easy, and makes what is said clear.

At this point you should sit back and think about what is being said, for in these few pages we have jumped from looking for something worth living for, to the suggestion that you search yourself for an understanding of love, to the idea that all people should love one another. If you have not searched your heart, mind, soul, your very being, and have not yet understood love, what we are saying may seem interesting but not profound.

We wish we could think of words and logical arguments that would make true, pure, real, love, crystal clear to you, but we can't. We are simply not talking about the kind of understanding that comes from reasoned analysis. We could fill these pages with elegant prose and poetry describing love, yet not one word would have the power or effect that even a fleeting inward glimpse of love has.

Your Best Is Good Enough

The following chapters will be very difficult to read and accept if you have not completed your search of your heart, mind, and soul. They represent logical conclusions as to what those who truly love can and should do. Love leads us to conclusions that may seem radical and simply wrong to those who do not know and understand love. You may think this can't be right, abandon your search, and reject what true, pure, love really is.

Please finish reading this book and the appendix before reaching your conclusions about love. As you read please do not reject what is said, complete your search, know and understand true, pure, real, love before you make your choices. Take all the time you need, days, weeks, months to search your heart, mind, and soul to know and understand love. Search your very being, until you know and understand what it means to love everyone with true, pure, real, love.

If you understand love you know loving does not require you to mechanically follow a set pattern of "right" actions. You know instead that if you love you will do the best you can in every situation, even if you cannot determine what the real solution is. If you love you do your best and doing your best is something you can always do. Doing your best simply requires that which you are capable of, nothing more.

This does not mean loving is any easier because you do not have to know what the "correct" answer is. On the contrary, to say love requires you to do your best is to say that love requires of you all you have to give. Love requires everything you can give, your total effort. By requiring only that which you are capable of giving, it is always your choice whether you love or don't love.

If you understand love you know it is your choice and your choice alone to love or not to love. If you love another human being you are giving that human being your very best. It is a profound responsibility to be able, every moment of your life, to love or not to love.

If you love every human being you are doing the very best you can do for each of them. Similarly, if they love you they are doing the very best they can for you. It is not hard to see that a world where each and every person loves each and every other person would be the best possible world. Since each of us can love if and when we want to love, a world filled with love is very much a possibility. Pure love is so rare a quantity in daily life it may seem almost impossible that, if they are willing to, each human being can love every other human being. Yet they can. We can bring about a world filled with love, a world that is worth living for.

Few of us seriously expect to see a day on earth when all people love one another. There are too many people for whom physical pleasure is more desirable than love. Only the most optimistic hold hope for a world filled with love.

In the next few chapters we will discuss physical pleasures. When we talk about physical pleasure (or just pleasure), even if we do not specifically include emotional pleasures, we mean both the physical and emotional pleasures we may seek when we do not love. We include both choices which maximize physical and emotional pleasure, and choices which minimize negative feelings and outcomes (like someone who drinks to avoid emotional pain). We include every choice to do anything other than give true, pure, real, love to others.

So what is the next best world? If you understand love you know you can love people even if they do not love you. You can always choose to love, and if love is the best you can do does it not seem true that you should love even if you are not loved? Does it not seem true that you should always choose love?

If life ends with physical death, perhaps the proper response to hate would not be love but would be some form of resistance to hate that minimizes its influence on others. Yet that cannot be true if our conclusions are right. Even though we cannot be certain, we have already explained why we believe that if existence ends with physical death nothing we do really matters at all so any response, or no response, would be equally acceptable. Indeed, as we discussed in earlier chapters, if existence does end with physical death the nothing that follows death means that any response will be as if it never was. What if life continues after death, would it matter what we do when faced with hate?

If life exists beyond the grave, and if love is the best part of life in this world, does it not seem logically and intuitively likely that if life after death is to be good it will be an existence filled with love? Of course we are dealing with questions beyond human ability to answer, we are in fact in the murky area where intellect, insight, and intuition blend with belief and faith.

There is no way at all we can say anything concrete about what life after death may or may not be like. Yet there exists a feeling that at least a portion of whatever lies beyond the grave, if anything, possesses the positive characteristics of life in this world. If we come to believe the most positive aspect of life is love, then it somehow seems intuitively true that if those who choose to love on earth enter a life after death it will be a life that is filled with love.

So what is our answer? Who should you love? If loving is good, the question really becomes is there anyone you should not love? If you understand love you know you can always love someone even if the person you love hates you. When you hate those who hate you, you are doing the same wrong to them they are doing to you.

The natural reaction is to hate those who hate you. Yet when you hate those who hate you, you are rejecting love. If you understand love you should, after deep thought and consideration, reach the conclusion that since you never have to choose hate you should always choose love (in the Appendix we discuss if we should love someone who has totally rejected love).

What if the person who hates you continues to hate you and does all kinds of evil to you and to others without sign of remorse? Again, if you understand love you know you can always love another person even if that person hates you. If we agree that the best we can do in this life, and in a life after death if one exists, is to love each other, the answer seems clear. If it is your choice to love or not to love you should choose to love every moment of your earthly life. That means you should love even if you are not loved, even if you are hated.

If love is worth living for in this life, it is worth living for in whatever life may follow death. If it is possible that we continue to exist after death, it would seem that we should love now with the hope that when we die we will pass into a life where love will not only continue, but will be shared by all who join us there.

What Should I Do?

Does this mean you should never show any anger? If a child does something you know will hurt them, and those who love them, you will be disappointed and "angry" at both their actions and perhaps at them. Yet anger that accompanies love is far different than anger that comes from hate and is perhaps not anger at all. Such anger is in fact a deep and emotional concern for people which seeks to bring a person back to love. The anger of a person who loves passes quickly, and forgiveness is freely and repeatedly given. If you understand love you know that if you love someone who hates you, you will forgive them each time they wrong you.

Loving someone does not mean you should support the wrongs they do. Many people who love others and try to help them out of problems like gambling, drinking, casual sex, etc., find themselves defending the other person and slipping into their way of life. There is a fine line between being with people and loving and helping them and, in an attempt to reach them, accepting at least part of their way of life. If at all times you keep in your heart, mind, and soul what it means to truly love you will have no trouble knowing where that line is.

If you want to love you must search your very being for the answers love requires and you must be willing to accept without change the answers you find. You are driving home from work, heading for a birthday party your spouse and friends have been planning for you. Traffic is heavy on the freeway. You see a man hitchhiking, he seems unsure of his footing, as you get closer you can tell he is drunk. If you stop you are sure to be late for your party, anyway, there are lots of cars one of which is bound to pick him up, and he doesn't look like he will stagger into the roadway.

You think, "he may be pretending to be drunk so he can rob somebody, a policeman is bound to drive by, I can call one on my mobile phone". Time to decide what to do. You want to drive on by him and not have to decide, but you know you have to stop or not stop. You stop your car, help the man into the passenger seat, he mumbles the town he is going to and then passes out. You try to call your spouse but get the answering machine. When you reach the right exit you get off and try to rouse your passenger. He gets sick and throws up, you stop to let him get some air and to clean out the car.

You're forty minutes late for your party and your spouse is still not answering. You think about leaving him at a gas station, but you help him back in the car and go on. He sees a bar, yells for you to stop, and curses you when you don't. You arrive in his hometown but he is too drunk to remember where he lives. You find a motel, get the hitchhiker a room, and pay the desk clerk to look in on him to see he is all right and to bring him breakfast the next morning. You buy him some clean clothes and put them in the room.

You call home, your spouse answers and then slams the phone down. Finally you arrive home three hours late, your guests have gone, your spouse and kids are mad, you are hungry and cold. You think about all the hassle you went through; the party you missed, your party; the drunk hitchhiker cursing you. You think, I hope I never get into another situation like this one, but if I do, I'll do it all over again. If you have not completed your search you may not understand the love given the hitchhiker. If you have, you know that if you choose love you would do the same things the driver did (we discuss difficult decisions in the Appendix – A Fanatic Life or a Normal Life).

If you love someone, whether they are your child or a stranger, you will do the very best you can for them. If you love someone you will do the best you can every moment of your life, even if it means that you do not have enough to meet your own needs. You will have compassion for every human being who does not have enough to eat and you will invite them to eat with you. You will care for those who are sick until they get well. If you meet someone who is homeless you will find shelter for them.

You will spend time with those who are lonely, and you will listen to their problems. You will be a companion to the elderly who will not get well. You will console those whose minds are troubled. You will gladly sacrifice your comfort so that others may have the best possible physical and emotional life. You will be filled with joy when their lives are filled with love. You will help them not because it makes you feel good, but because you love them. You will give them the love that is in your heart, mind, and soul.

Sit back and think and think and think about loving people with true, pure, real, love. Take all the time you need to feel and experience the love inside you that you can give to all people. Complete your search of your heart, mind, and soul and know and understand love.

You choose love, that means everything is all right, right? In a very real sense the answer to that question is yes, for you everything is all right. Everything being all right does not, however, mean that your life on earth will be physically better. Probably it will get much worse, for those who choose not to love will be doubly hard on those who do.

If you love someone you will not hit them when they strike you. You will give them food, and drink, and shelter even if they hate you and even if you end up not having enough for yourself. If you love them you will help them when they are sick, even if they have cheated you and cursed your stupidity. You will love them no matter what they do to you with the knowledge that you are doing what all human beings can and should do.

Forgiveness

Either you love or you do not love, if you love you are doing that which is right and good and if you do not love you are doing that which is wrong and bad. Good is good and bad is bad. We are not about to suggest all wrongs are equal, that cheating on an exam is as bad as murdering somebody, that watching an x-rated movie is as bad as rape, or that yelling at your spouse is as bad as beating them. What we do suggest is that all are bad. If you understand love you know if you choose to love you will do what you can do, you will do that which is good for people and not that which is bad. If one person is guilty of cheating and another is guilty of murder it is in fact profoundly true that both have done wrong.

Yet no-one loves all their lives, everyone chooses to give in to temptations sometime, even if it means just a quick look at a sex magazine or telling a lie to stay out of trouble. It may seem unfair but once done even the slightest wrong can never be undone (since we always have a choice it really is not unfair). You cannot uncheat a test, unmurder a victim, take back an argument, undo an affair, etc., etc., etc. We have, each and every one of us, done wrong. From the moment we commit our first wrong it is clear that we can never return to the state of having done no wrong.

We have said you can choose to love any time you want to. This is true no matter what you have done in the past and only requires that you want to love now. If you decide to love what can you do about your past? The only thing that can be done is that you can be forgiven for having not loved. If you understand love, you know that if you love someone you will forgive them the wrongs they have done to you.

Think carefully about love and forgiveness, and you will understand that if you love someone you will always and repeatedly and truly forgive them for having not loved you. You will forgive the liar, the cheat, the thief. You will forgive the rapist, the murderer, the child molester. When you understand love you will know that if you love someone you will forgive them for everything they do to you and to other people (we discuss one possible exception in the Appendix where the other person has rejected love).

The murderer who admits his wrong and seeks forgiveness is perhaps better off than the cheat who denies he has done anything wrong and rejects any thoughts about needing forgiveness. If we have all done wrong and if those who love forgive, we should not keep score of each person's wrongs we should forgive them. If you love people, you will forgive them. No matter how many times they may ask you to forgive them, if they seek your forgiveness and you love them, you will forgive them.

We are not saying that every person who seeks forgiveness is sincere, perhaps most are not. We are not suggesting that forgiving someone who has murdered means giving them a gun, or that forgiving someone who has been abusive means leaving them alone with children. Indeed, if we love both the one who has done harm and their victims we will do what we can to prevent future harm to either of them. We are saying that if you love both you will tell them about love and help them do that which is good so that they will want to love and will want to give and receive forgiveness.

It is clear that if someone loves you and seeks your forgiveness you can and should love them, and out of that love you will forgive them. No matter how many times they may ask you to forgive them, if they seek your forgiveness and you love them you will forgive them.

What about those people who don't want your forgiveness? If you have completed your search and know and understand love you know and understand that if someone is your enemy and hates you, you can and should love them. If you love people who hate you and do not want forgiveness you will love them and do good to them with the hope that they will choose to love you and seek forgiveness.

You can and should love both those who love you and seek forgiveness, and love those who hate you and do not seek forgiveness. To love those who hate you and who laugh at your forgiveness is perhaps the greatest test of your desire to love.

War or Peace

What if the choice comes whether to kill someone or be killed by them? We cannot see how a person could choose to intentionally kill someone they love. Let us simply say it seems to us that if you continue to exist after death, and if it is true that if you love someone you will never kill them, then you have nothing to fear if because you love you die and enter an existence filled with love.

One of the strange threads of lovelessness that runs through human history is the cruelty of war. Leaders and their led have, from the ancient days of Viking conquest through the mindless cruelty of Hitler to the countless deaths from hundreds of mini wars going on today to gang warfare in the streets, inflicted the most horrendous tortures on their fellow human beings. The choice of war is perhaps best explained as a choice of power, riches, and the perverse pleasures of pain.

It is simple to define a group as an enemy, be they another nation, race, or merely a group of people with whom you disagree and who seem threatening to you. For those who choose the physical pleasures of power over love, the conversion of human beings into the enemy, and from an enemy into inanimate targets, is simple and automatic. Perhaps it is accompanied by some form of logical argument such as freeing of the oppressed, protecting the innocent, creation of a master race, etc. Perhaps it is supported by a vocal cadre of men, women, and children urging on the conquest of the infidel, the bourgeois, the communist, etc. Whatever the rationale, the bad guy is defined, the good guy is identified, and the war is on.

The view of the enemy depends a great deal on the reason for the war. Initiators of the confrontation may see themselves as breaking the bonds of economic oppression, and thus "love" the victims but hate their leaders. They may see themselves as protectors of freedom, or religious soldiers, or any other manner of noble warrior who hates no one and who kills only so others may live. Or they may see themselves as simple killers whose mercenary skills are listed on employment applications. Each of these groups, no matter what the rationale, kills people.

Soldiers sometimes adopt intense devotion to their own families, as though they receive some cooling balm from those relationships that makes their violence toward others less real. The intensity of "love" of family that accompanies combat is a prelude to the destruction of true love that is the inevitable result of war. Though it may appear love plays some part in the motivation for fighting, by its very nature love can only be a victim of warfare.

For those who understand love, it is not hard to condemn war as the opposite of love. It is less easy, however, to condemn the deterrence or containment of war. If, for example, the presence of nuclear arms prevents a war, can such weaponry be a tool of peace? Can someone threaten to destroy an entire nation out of love for its inhabitants? The answer must come from your understanding of love.

What does appear true to us is that humankind will always have among it human beings whose choice of physical pleasures will lead them to war. The person who espouses disarming must accept that the consequence of doing so may literally be the death and/or subjugation of the majority of the human race. Indeed, the elimination of the nuclear weapons umbrella might return the world to confrontations between troops armed with conventional weapons that would kill and maim millions.

On the other hand, a world without weapons might be a world at peace. We are not suggesting that there could ever be a reason for actually using nuclear weapons as opposed to the maintenance of a peacekeeping bluff. Nor are we suggesting love does not require an absolute rejection of use of any violence as we believe it does. What we are saying is that if we are to be honest with ourselves we know that if we reject violence even in self-defense we must accept that the possible consequences may include death and subjugation.

You never have to commit any violent act against another, it is always your choice to do so or not. If love requires rejection of all violence against another human being, as we believe it does, those who understand love should understand it is worth enduring pain in this life if accepting such pain leads to love, both now and in whatever existence follows death. Death followed by a joyful eternal life of love, day after day, year after year, millions of years after millions of years, forever and ever and ever and ever, seems far superior to a pleasant life followed by a loveless eternity. We need to remember that no matter how hard we try to avoid our inevitable deaths the fact is that we live lives that are no more than single grains among the infinite sands of time.

If love is right, even one decision not to love is wrong. When you complete your search perhaps you may not agree with us that you will never inflict physical harm on someone you love. The answer you find to this question, and other questions less dramatic but as hard or harder to answer, is to be found in your knowledge and understanding of love.

After you have completed your search, and know and understand love, you will have to decide for yourself whether or not our answer to the question about killing, as well as our answers to many other difficult questions, are based on love, or not (we discuss difficult choices in the Appendix). We believe they are, but perhaps they are not. We believe that after you complete your search of heart, mind, and soul you will know and understand that if anything is true, it is true that every moment of their lives each and every human being can and should love each and every other human being.

There is no question in our hearts, minds, and souls that every person should love every other person. Indeed, if every person chose to love every other person as they would have those people love them, if every person chose to love every other person as himself or herself, then each of us would do the very best that we could do for every human being in the world. There would be nothing more that we should do for each other, nothing more that we could do.

One essential warning, when faced with a hard question the normal human response is toward self-interest, with elaborate arguments to justify the answer and make it seem to be the result of love. The answer dictated by love is often (for some people almost always) very, very, hard to accept. Yet we are convinced that if you choose love you will accept the toughest of answers and will find peace and hope in your decisions. At all times you must be absolutely certain that your answers are based on the knowledge and understanding of love you find in your heart, mind, and soul. You must be certain that you always choose true, pure, real, love.

Each moment of hate is a moment when you could have chosen love. If love is best, what could possibly be better than choosing to love every moment of your earthly life?

Men, Women, & Love

If you listen to people talking about love between men and women you will quickly find that the love they describe may have only a slight, or even no, resemblance to the love you found when you searched your heart, mind, and soul. Many men and women sincerely believe love is a physical attraction between the sexes that somehow magically appears, must be cultivated by keeping the partner interested, and sometimes simply fades away. From the rush of adrenaline and the pounding heart which accompanies puppy love, to the passionate emotions of the "perfect" affair, most of humankind accepts, and in fact welcomes, pleasant feelings of sexual thoughts and deeds.

All manner of sexual experiences are accepted without question. From the "innocent" enjoyment of a beauty contest, to the pleasures of casual sex, to unbelievable perversions, people enjoy whatever degree of sexual excitement their background and their "morals" will allow. Each of these indulgences is justified by some form of argument about sex being only natural and feeling good being all right.

Even those whose ideas about love and marriage are more traditional are often lulled into what, for lack of a better description, may be called romantic love. The intense emotions that accompany any relationship, plus the pressures of society, combine to push people into playing stereotypical roles of dating. Men and women do the best they can to be interesting to each other, to make each other have a good time, and particularly not to rock the romantic boat. A general fear of being unpopular, of losing favor with another person, of being an oddball, runs through most people's minds.

When a man and a woman fall into playing the game of love they lose their identity as people who can truly love each other. Even though they may think what they are feeling is love for one another it is more often infatuation with the romantic atmosphere and the idealized images of themselves they have created. The question is asked with increasing frequency, can a man and a woman really love each other for the rest of their lives?

Think a few minutes about the love you found when you searched your heart, mind, and soul. Then think about giving that love to another person, and in return being loved by them. If you truly understand love, you will understand that true love can exist between all people, and that true love between a man and a woman can exist. The love you find in your heart, mind, and soul is far more than physical attraction or magical moments. It is the ultimate, joyful relationship between people, where each person cares as much for the other person as for himself or herself. If you understand love, you know it is the deepest commitment one human being can give another.

If a man loves a woman, and a woman a man, when they look in each other's eyes they are not filled with lust, they are filled with love for each other. When their hands touch they are not filled with desire, they are filled with deep feelings of love. When they are with each other they know their love will not fade but will truly last their lifetimes. If they decide they want to spend the rest of their lives together as husband and wife they may choose to marry and have children.

Some readers will throw their hands up and exclaim what simplistic mishmash this is, life is nowhere near as easy as that, nor are human relationships that simple. Those who understand love know that what we are describing is far from simplistic. If you truly understand love, you will understand that the love we are describing is the basis of the deepest and most profound relationship people can have. What makes these sentences sound naive and childish is the tendency of all of us to equate the word love with what we have been told love is. Novels, movies, poets, television, rock stars, friends, parents, teachers, have told us love is some sort of fragile entity which comes and goes with adversity and changes in the weather.

To people who only understand love in so limited and weak a form, the idea of deep and permanent love shared by two people seems a romantic absurdity. It is little wonder they find it almost impossible to believe true love can exist between a husband and a wife.

We are not suggesting sex is evil, indeed having a child is one of the strongest expressions of love between two people who have chosen to marry and live their lives together. What we are saying is that if people truly love each other they are not attracted to each other by desire for physical pleasure, they are brought together by love. When they are with each other, they have real, true, deep, love, in their hearts.

The biologic purpose of sex is the creation of new human life. Love between a husband and wife, conception and birth, and the giving of love to a child makes sexual intercourse far more than a physical act.

Sexual acts and relationships which are not for the purpose of the birth of a child, whether they are heterosexual, homosexual, autoerotic, or other ways of attaining physical pleasure, are filled with lust, not love. Lust destroys the love human beings can share. Men and women who seek physical and emotional pleasure from sex are not giving each other true love.

Having children is not only an expression of love between a man and a woman who choose to marry, it is an expression of love for the whole human race. When physical or emotional pleasure from sexual relations is one of the goals of a human relationship, the true love that a man and woman who choose to marry can share is lost. When a man and a woman, or for that matter two men or two women, seek physical or emotional pleasure from sexual relations they not only weaken their love for each other, they weaken their love for all people. Every act that has pleasure, not procreation, as its goal renders sex less than an expression of love and weakens our love of all people.

If you lust for someone your love for them will grow weaker and weaker as physical and emotional pleasure replaces love. If you love someone you will have love for them, not lust, in your heart, mind, and soul. It is hard to imagine how anyone could treat another person as someone they derive physical and emotional pleasure from and at the same time love other people as human beings. The dehumanizing effect of sex for physical and emotional pleasure extends beyond the moment and the relationship of the people involved, it follows them into their daily lives. Lust for even one person makes it difficult, or impossible, to love all people. Eventually those who seek physical and emotional pleasure from other people may not truly love anyone at all.

It is often difficult for people who have decided to marry to understand why it is wrong for them to express their love before marriage through sex. They see sex between two people who are truly committed to living with each other for the rest of their lives as being far different from sex between people whose commitment may be something less, or none at all. There is no question it is the commitment that unites two people and not marriage, yet marriage is more than a formality.

Marriage is the moment of final commitment when two people declare to themselves their love and their decision to become a family. By tradition it is the point in time when two people join together, yet more than tradition, it is when human beings who truly love one another know in their hearts that their commitment is complete. It is the single act of marriage that marks the combining of two lives.

Any physical joining between two people before this total commitment is complete weakens the bond of love between them. On their wedding day a person joins with someone they love. When two people have sex before this final expression of their commitment, the sex they enjoy is not part of the ultimate joining of two human beings.

Sex before marriage is something less than the final confirmation of the decision to give a lifetime of love to another person. It takes from people that one moment in their lives that should be the beginning of their marriage. Yet even if the moment is lost a husband and wife can still choose to give true, pure, real love to each other for the rest of their lives.

What about divorce? Again, the answer comes from truly understanding deep, real love. If a man and a woman choose to love each other and live their lives together, what can make them change their minds? So long as two people choose to love each other they will never part. Remember, what we are talking about is true, deep love, not that which is called love but is only a shadowy illusion which fades in the light of dawn. We are talking about the love a husband can always choose to give a wife, and a wife can always choose to give a husband, love many couples are not willing to share. A man or woman may separate from a spouse who does not love them yet remain hopeful that their spouse will love them again.

What about the millions of women and men who meet without any intention of marriage, what harm is there in the pleasure of a little sex among friends? The answer to that question is a difficult one that, at least for this and future generations, seems far harder to grasp than for previous generations. Indeed sex is not new, and perhaps casual sex was quietly practiced as much or more in the past as it is today, yet it was generally accepted that it was "not right". Today that idea has faded and for many sex has become a popular pastime.

The answer to the question of casual sex is not found in logical arguments or in medical reports extolling the mental and physical benefits of an active sex life. It is found in an understanding of love. If you truly understand love, you understand what it means for a man and a woman to choose to love each other and live together for their entire lives. If you understand love you know that when two people who are not married choose to have sex they are not choosing love.

Is it possible that if we choose to love all people we should choose not to marry? If we love a spouse the focus of much of our love will be turned toward them and away from other people. If we love a child we will focus our love on that child as we guide them through infancy to adulthood. We do not see how it is possible not to direct toward our spouse and child some of the love we would give to others if we did not have a spouse or child.

Indeed, it seems true that there is no harm done if we never marry, no harm done to a child who is never conceived, yet there is harm done by focusing our love on a spouse and child while other people need food, water, and our companionship. Our conclusion is that if you choose to love all people with the love that if it is to be given to one must be given to all, you should not marry. This is a very difficult conclusion, yet we believe that if you complete your search of your heart, mind, and soul, and know and understand love, you will understand the conclusion (in the Appendix we discuss living a "fanatic" life or a "normal" life).

If you do choose to marry, or you are already married, we believe you will also reach the conclusion we discussed earlier, you will not divorce. This may seem contradictory but it isn't. By choosing not to marry a person does not separate two people. However, if a person divorces his or her spouse they tear apart two people who already made the choice to be together for the rest of their lives.

What about the intense, passionate love we sometimes see between people which may drive one human being to heady, irrational, and total commitment to another human being, even to the point of deeply hurting friends, children, or spouses? We do not suggest the intensity of passionate "love" does not bring to its participants incredible pleasure, pleasure beyond the physical, pleasure which would perhaps be the goal of all humankind were it not for that which must be lost in gaining it. For even though we have tried and tried and tried and tried to imagine the coexistence of what we might call passionate love with that which we have called true love, it seems to us they cannot exist together in one human being. A person who chooses to give passionate love to another person cannot also choose to give true love to all people. Passionate love overwhelms true love, it demands that people do that which they would not do if they loved all people.

The love you will find when you search your heart, mind, and soul, love every person can give every other person, may not bring with it the emotional high passion offers, yet it is an all-consuming love which becomes part of a person's very being. Though it may lack the emotional fever that accompanies passionate romance the transformation that occurs when a human being chooses to love all people gives that person love which does not appear and disappear, brighten and fade. It is love that is with them and comforts them every moment of their lives. A love that does not focus its energy on one or two people, but rather a love that spreads out from a person and grows and strengthens as it radiates into the world. That love, whether it is called ideal or pure or true, or just called love, is more intense than any love we can imagine.

Indeed, while it is true that the love between people who love all other people is clearly different to the explosive passion of two lovers for whom the rest of the world does not exist, we believe it is in fact far more intense and beautiful and joyous. Only a man or a woman who gives real, pure, true love to all people can give real, pure, true love to each individual person. The person for whom love must be a passionate emotional experience shared by a few does not understand and cannot give to anyone the all-consuming love which we know and understand when we search our heart, mind, and soul. They have locked fellow human beings out of their hearts, minds, and souls and thus have lost the love that, if it is given to anyone, must be given to all.

What about the millions upon millions of people who most would conclude do not lust for each other, but who look at each other as being physically attractive, and who may flirt with each other? When the vast majority of people look at each other, at least to some extent they see each other as more or less physically attractive, as having a more or less pleasant personality, as being more or less desirable to be with. Far beyond the question of sexual attraction, most human beings will tell you that they get along better with people who exhibit compatible personality traits. Indeed, most people have a group of friends they enjoy being with and other groups of people they avoid. It seems that people like to be around people who make them feel good. Is there anything wrong with that?

If when you look at someone you are looking for something in them that makes you feel good, whether that may be innocent sexual attractiveness or delightful conversation or something else, you are not giving them the love that is in your heart, mind, and soul. If you love someone when you look at them you do not have thoughts about their physical appearance. If you love someone you do not think about what their personality is like. If you love someone you do not think about whether or not you want to be around them and be their friend. If you love someone you do not have thoughts about whether or not they make you feel good. If you love someone, when you look at them you have love for them in your heart, mind, and soul.

If you give someone true, pure, real, love, you will love them, and you will not think of them as someone you do or do not want to be around. You will love all people, including those who other people consider to be ugly or dull or stupid or inferior. When you look at them you will not see someone who is sexually attractive or vivacious or funny or popular, you will see someone you love. When you look at them you will not see someone who is ugly or dull or stupid or inferior, or anything else, you will see someone you love. If you give to everyone the true, pure, real, love that is in your heart, mind, and soul, they will be more than your friends, they will be your family who you love.

Why Do You Do What You Want to Do?

Why would anyone choose not to love? Why does a person show off his or her diamonds to friends who can't meet their house payments? Why do employees do everything they can to make sure they get a promotion instead of fellow workers? Why do people lie their way through tight spots, blaming their mistakes on someone else? Why do people read in the newspaper every cruel detail of a violent rape? Why does a person have an affair with someone else's wife? Why do they party through the night, drinking until they pass out? Why do they gamble away the family grocery money? Why do they periodically indulge themselves in their favorite form of orgy, sexual or otherwise?

Why do they rape? Why do they torture? Why do they kill? The questions are endless. The possibilities are as numerous as all the schemes and plots and cruelties and fantasies and perversions the human mind can imagine. The answers are as numerous. They range from "normal instinctive human behavior" to "environmentally aggravated hereditary mental disease". Those who shudder at the acts of someone else often offer explanations that seek to explain how people are led into aberrant behavior.

Each commentator tries to define and isolate the unacceptable behavior, whether it is some form of sexual perversion or shoplifting or murder. The behavior is seen as a clear deviation from the norm, which can be traced to childhood traumas, socioeconomic pressures, impressionable minds, etc. When other explanations prove absurd behavior is often attributed to the catchall "they must be crazy".

We are not prepared to reject the possibility that organic mental disease and non-physical psychological trauma, cause or contribute to most of the horrors of the world. In fact, researchers can bring on the most perverse behavior by artificially stimulating the brain with chemicals or electricity. However, we are convinced that the vast majority (perhaps all) of human behavior is not determined by external or internal forces acting on the mind, but rather by conscious human choice among more or less clear alternatives.

We are not saying biophysical urges to lie, cheat, gamble, drink, have sex, etc., do not exert incredible pressures to act and not think. We realize they are major factors on which we base our decisions. Nor are we saying peer group pressures and lifetime experiences unique to each person's surroundings (in the broadest sense, including teachers and relatives as well as peer groups) do not exert incredibly strong pressures. What we are saying is neither heredity nor environment nor a combination of both is adequate to explain human behavior.

If a person does not get pleasure from a perverse act, they will not do it. That basic common sense statement, however seemingly true it may appear, has fostered centuries of controversy. Early religious thinkers, and many humanistic philosophers as well, accepted the general proposition that each of us is in control of our behavior. Later generations of social scientists saw in such statements a sociopolitical attempt to justify repression of beliefs and lifestyles practiced by any group in a numerical and/or political minority. The researchers virtually ignored the idea that some sort of meaningful individual freewill process is involved in decision making and instead adopted a deterministic approach to human behavior which described nearly every human action in terms of heredity and environment.

We have already discussed the idea of human freewill, no one is going to prove freewill exists or that it does not. Your belief about your freewill ability to choose among alternatives is a question of what you believe, or have faith, is true. Yet even those scientists who would answer affirmatively if asked whether humans have freewill curiously take sides in the heredity vs environment controversy, as if freewill plays an insignificant role in decision making.

We believe both hereditary-physiological and environmental-psychological factors are real, and play a crucial, critical role in the human decision-making process. However, we believe the controversy over which is controlling misses the real point that neither are controlling. Each influence human beings to a degree that varies from individual to individual.

Perhaps many individuals who do not understand such influences are affected to the extent their decisions become virtually automatic, perhaps not. Regardless of the relative strengths of hereditary and environment on human beings we believe the controlling factor in the human decision-making process is the illusive freewill choice. Those who seem to respond automatically to hereditary and environmental pressures do so simply because they have not chosen to do otherwise.

While a significant number of scientists champion various forms and degrees of determinism, we doubt that the majority would argue strongly against the proposition of freewill ability to alter conduct. For one thing to do so virtually takes away any claim of uniqueness for the human species, the species of which all scientists are members. For another, there appears to exist deep within us a feeling of control over our decisions. That feeling does not prove you can make freewill choices, but it does not weaken any faith or belief we may have in the existence of freewill.

Since we have said we cannot prove or disprove the existence of freewill, the fact you feel a sense of ultimate control should tend to strengthen your belief in freewill and is as positive evidence for such belief as you are likely to find. So, is the answer to the question "why do people do what they do" simply that they do what they want to do? With the possible exception of those driven by compulsions truly beyond their ability to control, if such compulsions actually exist, the simple answer is people do what they want to do, whether their goal is to maximize positive physical pleasure, minimize negative emotions, or accomplish some other outcome. If you agree, as we do, with those who believe that people have the freewill ability to make choices and decisions, you should have little problem agreeing that if you have a choice to do or not to do something harmful to another person, and doing it does not further some objective you have, you will not do it.

But how can anyone want to rape or kill somebody? Even the most sheltered human beings experience, at some time and to some degree, the feelings of physical pleasure that come from sexual fantasies, dreams of wealth, desires to beat an opponent to a pulp. Most of us have led less sheltered existences and, to varying degrees, know the pleasure of being slightly drunk, of winning the daily double, of an x-rated movie. The list of physical pleasures is long, and for some the degree of intensity of pleasure associated with them seems to increase as their acceptability in society goes down. Yet you know that most people could get no satisfaction from a violent or perverse act, how then can human beings who do violence to other human beings enjoy what they do? The answer lies in the absolute opposite natures of love and, what for want of any better description, we call physical pleasure.

When you love somebody the last thing you want to do is hurt them. You may choose to "love" some people but use others for your own pleasure. That pleasure may be sexual, or perhaps may be the feeling of power that can come from being boss and master, or may be any other pleasure that is enjoyed at someone else's expense. You choose physical pleasure when you do any of the millions of possible acts you would not do if you loved people. As you love fewer and fewer people and give less love to those people you do love, you get further and further and further away from love.

Even though we may leave love behind, most of us never get so far away that we no longer feel the physical and emotional pain which goes with not loving others. When two people who have lost sight of love get together they may enjoy physical pleasures with only a slight and distant feeling something is missing and wrong. Yet for those people there is always a limit to the pain they will inflict on another human being. They may not realize such a limit exists, but it does, and it results in their pleasure being cut off by the increasing emotional or physical pain of others.

Yet some choose to go so far in their quest for physical pleasure that love becomes distant, unknown, and unwanted. Among those who choose such an existence are people who seek only their own pleasure, pleasure that not only does not diminish but is enhanced by the pain of others.

When love becomes a word without meaning to someone, people that they meet are no longer people, they are literally objects, deserving no more than an animal. As more and more people become like animals to a person so too the one who dehumanizes is dehumanized. No one can continue to consider himself or herself to be something unique if they consider others as objects of pleasure. Such people, unhampered by feelings of love, can do virtually anything that gives them physical pleasure without any remorse for the pain inflicted on fellow "animals".

It is hard for people who may not truly love, but who have not come close to abandoning love, to understand the physical pleasures of rape, murder, and all the other horrible perversions imaginable. Yet everyone should realize that people who have virtually abandoned love, and thus have almost no limits on their actions, actually do get pleasure from the perverse. If they did not get pleasure from their acts they would not do them. (Beyond the people who have distanced themselves from love, are those who have totally rejected and abandoned love, they are discussed in the Appendix.)

114

Again what we have said comes with the caveat that among those people who are unable to control some of their actions perhaps there exists a group of people who cannot choose not to harm others. One can never be sure how many, if any, fall in that group. Since most of us retain at least some of our sensitivity to the pain of others we tend to label as "crazy" anyone who acts without regard to such pain.

Perhaps some people are compelled to do that which harms others, perhaps not. Perhaps (as we believe) everyone, including those who are "crazy", can choose love, perhaps not. What we can say is that those who harm others and who are not crazy choose to do whatever brings them the physical pleasure they seek with conscious, reasoned contempt for the pain of others.

We should emphasize that we are in no way suggesting that those who have distanced themselves from love but not totally rejected it cannot reverse course and choose love. Indeed those people who are engaged in perverse human depravities, but who have not totally rejected love, may at any time choose to love people for the remainder of their lives. Conversely, many who would never dream of committing rape may choose to continue to enjoy newspaper accounts of rapes, never losing sight of what love is, yet never choosing to love.

Those people continue to be what the former rapist was. What we are trying to emphasize is that people choose not to love not because loving makes them feel bad, but because the alternative to loving is physical pleasure which is real and intense and lasting. Those who think that people who choose the perverse don't know what they are doing are kidding themselves. Most, if not all, have made a conscious decision to enjoy physical and emotional pleasures at the expense of love. Anyone who wants to understand the millions of people who do millions of acts against love needs to remember those acts give them pleasure. They also need to realize that as long as we live in a hedonistic world such pleasures will continue to be real, intense, and available to all who choose to enjoy them.

As long as you are busy with the normal routines of life such pleasures seem remote and less than real. If you risk getting closer to the pleasures you will find yourself beginning to tingle with an unexpected but pleasant sense of anticipation. If you let yourself go you will literally be engulfed in a whirlpool of rapidly intensifying feelings that draw you deeper and deeper into mindless enjoyment of the moment.

Those who have not regularly experienced the electricity of physical pleasure, or who might not anticipate the power of a particular experience, are likely to find themselves alternately condemning the moment and wanting it to be more intense. They might justify their actions by promising themselves they will reform immediately after this time; by declaring they are too weak to resist; or, even worse, by asserting that some intellectual insight shows them the overall desirability of their behavior.

It should be noted that those who have experienced the depths of physical pleasures usually describe a sort of disappointment, emptiness, or other negative feeling which over time invades their bliss. This feeling of loss is combated by shaking it from their minds with the help of drugs or alcohol or mind-blanking self-induced euphoria, or by doing a little something different, or by going just a little bit further.

At one time or another most people choose physical enjoyment over love and some live their entire lives for pleasure. Yet most carry with them an understanding of the dark side of physical pleasure that is an inseparable part of such pleasures. Someone who toys with those pleasures may only glimpse the darkness that accompanies them and may indeed be able to ignore the feeling that something is wrong. In fact, they may be able to deaden their feelings of love so much that they live their entire lives enjoying physical pleasures while ignoring the inevitable destruction of their lives, as well as the lives of those around them.

The enjoyment of physical pleasures is far more pervasive than most people recognize. Consider the fact that newspapers seldom detail a burglar's entry into a home or the details of a simple traffic ticket, but practically always go into great detail about rapes and murders. For example, the extreme detail in news reports about wars and war machines? That detail, of course, is not accidental. Regardless of claims of news value it serves no other purpose than to provide a source of perverse, supposedly harmless, physical pleasure for the reader. Just as the act itself is harmful the pleasant feelings of morbid curiosity are also harmful.

Even if the majority of members of the society in which we live profess a belief in religion it seems that the overall trend is toward a more humanistic, secular world. For many taboos of past decades have become marginally acceptable, everyday events. Every decade the lyrics of songs are more sexual, the videos increasingly violent, the jokes raunchier, the content of life more "adult" oriented. We gradually push the

116

boundaries of behavior to incorporate what was unacceptable so that we can justify our desire for more and more physical pleasures.

Those who fantasize about sexual pleasures, perhaps watching an R rated movie or a pro-football half time, are rejecting love as surely as someone who is having an affair with his neighbor's wife. People who read newspaper or television accounts about wars and crimes and greed and power are choosing physical pleasure over love. Human beings who choose television, movies, and video games that contain sex and violence choose physical pleasure instead of love.

Love does not come from a person's acts and deeds but from inside their heart, mind, and soul. If a person is filled with love their thoughts will be thoughts of love and their deeds will be deeds of love. We are not suggesting evil thoughts do not cross the minds of those who love, what we are saying is that such thoughts are not welcomed by them. Nor are we suggesting it is no worse to have an affair than it is to see an R rated movie, what we are saying is that those who love do neither.

Just as it is not right to kill someone it is not right to fantasize about killing someone who wrongs you. Just as it is not right to have sexual relations with someone for physical and emotional pleasure it is not right to replace thoughts of love with sexual fantasies. Fantasies of lust and power and money replace feelings of love with dreams of physical and emotional pleasure, weakening the love between people. Thoughts about physical and emotional pleasures, sexual or otherwise, are the opposite of thoughts of love, and crowd more and more love out of our heart, mind, and soul.

If you have searched your heart, mind, soul, your very being, and know and understand love, you know that choosing physical pleasure is the opposite of choosing love. If and when you truly know and understand love you will understand that choosing physical pleasure destroys love. Each moment that you choose physical pleasure could have been a moment that you chose love. When you truly know and understand love you will know and understand that you should always choose love.

You're Not Normal If You Think I'm Not Normal

What about those people who go through life just living? One of the great mistakes in life is to focus attention on those who openly indulge in the perverse, or obviously hedonistic, pleasures of life, while giving only fleeting attention to the vast majority of people who live in that quiet, almost invisible world of normalcy. Within this great mass of humanity lies the borderline between love and no love. The boundary separating these two groups divides not only those who occupy the extremes of life but also marks the real and absolute division between those whose love, or lack of love, is hidden by daily living.

Whether or not a clear and visible line can be discerned by people, we believe there is a real and absolute division so that at every moment in your life it is true you are either a member of the group that loves or you belong to the group that does not love. If it is your choice to love or not then making that choice determines at every moment which group you belong to. Though some disagree, we believe those who understand love know that the borderline exists, even if it is beyond human ability to locate.

Either you choose to love and belong to the group that loves, or you do not choose to love and belong to the group that does not love. This is not to say that passage between groups is restricted during your lifetime, for it appears it is not. If we are to continue to assume it is your choice to love or not to love then passage among the groups depends on that choice, and is apparently prohibited only to those who have totally rejected love.

At any one point in time, and thus every moment of our lives, we either love or we do not love. Many variations of this proposition of a division between people exist, including ideas about a purgatory from which escape is possible even after death. While the groups are described differently by different cultures and religions, most end up as two clear, separate and distinct masses which sometime after death are forever fixed and unchanging (in the Appendix we discuss if those who reject love choose the group before physical death).

The vast majority of normal people appear to give little thought as to which group they belong to. They seem rather indifferent to the presence among them of the borderline, yet the existence of the line and their choice of sides determines the very nature of their being. A normal person exists among a huge mass of fellow normal people who embrace, protect, and shield him or her from the world around them. The peer group discourages thoughts and concerns about what the members as a whole stand for, what the individual really believes in, and where the group is headed.

The routines of daily life that guide a normal person (and guide you if you are normal) appear to be one of the strongest anesthetics of all time. The products of a normal person's labors include responsible corporate positions, attractive suburban houses, sensible cars, extensive charitable activities, active participation in church affairs, union membership, solid family ties, etc. All contribute to the individual's feeling that they are comfortably situated among, and a solid member of, the normal people of the world.

The output of the normal person's mind bombards his or her fellow human beings through newspapers, televisions, movies, books, conversations, advertisements, social media, etc., with the message that the normal person's values, behavior, likes, dislikes, ideas, and lifestyles, are not only acceptable, but are right, good, normal, healthy, and desirable. As each member moves through familiar streets, shops, offices, and homes the whole structure of normal society reinforces a belief that they and their peers are the foundation and strength of the society of which they are a part. Each reflection of the normal life, as seen by every member as they look at other members, solidifies their belief that they are what they should be.

To do that which is not normal brings immediate reaction from those around you. To persist in doing that which is the exception and not the rule focuses all the pressure society can bring to bear on the rebellious member. If a member's public behavior does not rapidly conform to at least the minimum requirements of normalcy they find themselves outside the group, which seems to huddle closely together and shrink from them with the intention of not only banning them forever but their ideas as well. With the increase of tolerance in modern society this process has become muted and less obvious, however it is still a basic tool of society. While friendships may now be tolerated among normal people and outcasts, the bond of membership remains coldly and cruelly destroyed.

A curious state of mind accompanies normal life, it is as if a restful, peaceful cloud surrounds and deadens human feelings, isolating each person from every other person's problems. A day may be spent with a normal amount of concern for others, even with a few shining moments of human compassion interspersed among scheduled routines. Yet the cloud of normalcy engulfs the mind and senses, making those moments no more than rare attempts at loving. The sense of people loving people is missing.

The frightening thing about normalcy is that it carries with it a sense of right which is the logical result of the sequence of intense socializing pressures that accompany normal growth. This myopic view of life is virtually devoid of the influence of love. Even worse is the conviction of most normal people who have not searched their heart, mind, and soul to understand love that they not only know what it means to love, but that they are indeed loving, caring individuals. The narcotic effect of normalcy renders those who do not throw aside the strong beliefs instilled by years of normal living and replace them with an understanding of love, slaves of their perfectly logical but loveless lives.

Though you may find it difficult to comprehend, all manner of philosophical beliefs from Nazi fascist superiority to Marxist revolution, right-wing militaristic conservatism to left wing social upheaval, sexual liberation to fanatic isolation of women from society, all can be argued for, intelligently supported, and devotedly engaged in by people who have total conviction in the rightness of their ideas and acts. Indeed, a normal person often exhibits unquestioning acceptance of the "goodness", and perhaps even superiority, of their group's values and life-style.

General beliefs and traditions of whatever group or groups one identifies with (whether ethnic, social, political, economic, intellectual or otherwise) mold, and may distort, the personal ideas each of us spend lifetimes developing and nurturing. Group ideas are so much a part of our lives that they become for us truths which we not only must live by, but which we are duty bound to defend and propagate. Group beliefs are absorbed by individual minds so that each of us lives our life, more or less intensely according to the nature of our beliefs, as if we and the other members of our group are the only ones who know how life should be lived.

There is another kind of pressure to conform to a normal routine, an internal pressure that few of us recognize. Each of us inherits millions of biological traits from our parents, who in turn inherited millions of traits from their parents. Some of us inherit better math skills, some greater artistic ability, some more athletic dexterity. Some of us are from birth, calmer, more emotional, faster, slower, smarter, musically inclined. As clearly as our environment is an external definition for us of a normal world, our heredity is an internal definition of a normal world. For many this inherited normal world can be a stronger anesthetic than the normal world offered by a somewhat detached environment.

Many, many people live their lives, from birth to death, blindly following the path that heredity provides for them. Those who are more emotional may be easily angered and lash out at family members, those who are less emotional may be apathetic toward the needs of others. Each person who follows the hereditary forces at work within them feels that they are doing what they do because they are who they are.

For most, it is far more difficult to recognize that they are intentionally following an ancient biologic roadmap than it is to simply believe that they are just being themselves. Indeed, many deny that they are like their parents only to eventually see an image of their parents' lives when they look in the mirror. They fail to realize and admit to themselves that in many ways they are willing clones of their ancestors.

Yet the traits that we inherit are just that, they are traits that cause us to have a tendency to make certain choices. While our hereditary traits may exert incredible internal pressure on us to make particular choices, the choices we make are none-the-less our own freewill choices. Our choices are not automatic, they are not determined by our environment or heredity unless we allow them to be. Our choice to follow our environmental or hereditary path is our freewill choice not to do otherwise.

If environment or heredity dictate our choice it is because we have not been willing to recognize the influence of our surroundings and our biologic heritage, and because we have not been willing to make our own freewill choices that transcend both environment and heredity. Admittedly, it may be incredibly hard not to follow the path our environment and heredity dictates for us, yet it is clear that we can make our own freewill choices, we can make our own path.

We have criticized normalcy as if it was a universal plague whose victims are unaware of the pain it inflicts. There is another way of looking at it. We can view normalcy as model behavior determined by a more or less democratic combination of biologic, environmental, intellectual, and other characteristics of human existence. What is normal is normal because it works best in the given situation.

For example, the normal routine for a particular office worker is adapted from time tested routines for similarly situated employees. It is followed by a worker not only because his or her ability to perceive alternatives has been numbed, but also because the normal routine serves them well. Thus, when we suggest you break free from the restraints of normalcy it is very important that you be committed to understanding love. For if you do not replace your normal routine with true love you will have simply given up the companionship and comfort of normal people for some lonely individualism, which in the long run will prove no better for you.

Perhaps most of us need a degree of normalcy where we follow routines that add stability to our lives. While it is wrong to hide among the majority of normal people who blend into the group to avoid doing what is right, it does not follow that one must stand apart from the crowd. There is certainly nothing wrong in being with people. Being distant and cold, separating yourself from society, is the opposite of loving.

It is one thing to be alone because you are the only person in a group who is willing to love, but it is quite the opposite to be alone because you are afraid or unwilling to love. What is required is that you love people with the hope that they will join together in a community where it is normal to love. To help build such a normal existence filled with love for all, whether or not you succeed, should be your goal.

Lonely Islands in a Sea of Normalcy

Individualism is in many ways the opposite of being a member of a group of normal people. The more isolated and sheltered we are from people while growing up, whether by barriers erected by protective parents or by our own fears or personality, the more likely we are to expect our lives and the people in them to behave according to an individual plan we construct in our minds. The greater our separation from people the more we transform them into characters in plays we author in our minds, expecting each person we meet to take their place in our script and to faithfully play the role we have written for them.

For the vast majority, on opening night or soon thereafter, the players get restless, the lines muddled, and the show slides downhill like a melodrama that just won't work. As the story starts to fall apart we find the fault to be with others. The simple problem is every actor is also a writer, and writers never write the same story.

People who grow up close to other people learn at an early age that very few do what people expect them to do, no matter how right or good it may seem. Those who understand the complexities of human beings are not surprised when things go totally opposite to what they plan and want. The many, many people who for some reason have not been close enough to others to really understand this are at the very least repeatedly hurt, and at worst devastated, by the "failure" of others. They often seek solitude and peace in an individualistic world of dream lovers and dream successes, a world where what they want to happen does happen.

Anyone who thinks only a few people fit that description does not realize that the world of dreams can be as subtle as the escape offered by television, movies, books, and particularly, as subtle as acceptance of the rhythm of daily lives filled with repetitious normal patterns of living. Just as being normal can make us part of a group, a veneer of normalcy can help us hide within a group, relieve us from the need to get to know other people, and protect us from hurt and disappointment. Some will never wake from their individual dreams, others will be awakened only to find themselves in the nightmare of a loveless reality they never dreamed existed.

Is escape all that bad? Without some release from reality the pressures of living would perhaps be too great for all but a few. Yet if we are to bring love into our lives we cannot ignore the very real obstacles to love that can only be dealt with in the harsh reality of life. Someone who is always looking for a romantic prince or princess will reject the real people around them who bring with them some pain, but who also are people the person can love and be loved by.

To hold back waiting for the storybook ending is to abandon the real, pure, and true love you can choose to give to people, and to reject the love, however imperfect, people are willing to give you. If we are to be more than observers of life we cannot seek only those who are perfect, for we will almost certainly never find anyone who is perfect. We must love people, even if we are not loved, and be willing to accept the inevitable and repeated rejection and defeat of a real world where love plays but a small part.

It would be great if we could tell you that it is likely this world will someday become a world filled with people loving people, but we can't. Love is the guiding force for only a few, a multitude of other goals control most lives. Often those who would choose love if they understood the choice are prisoners of their lack of understanding.

What about those who understand and choose love, what can we expect from them? Those who understand love and choose to love you now may, at some time in the future, choose not to love you. This leaves us with the possibility of a world filled with forgiving love that does not demand perfection, yet even that love is rarely seen.

Perhaps the best we can ever expect is a world where each of us is willing to recognize and accept that life is filled with imperfections and hatred and cruelties and loneliness, yet also recognize and accept that no matter what the world is like each of us can choose to love. A world where some choose to love, while others do not, is not an easy one to live in, yet given the nature of human existence it is the best we can expect.

Many of those who say they love you don't and are eventually going to hurt you. Some who love you one minute will choose not to love you the next, but that rejection of love is part of human behavior. It does not have to be, but it is, and it will continue to be so as long as people choose among all the multitude of pleasures that compete against love. No matter what other people do, whether they love you or not, you can always choose to love them. When you understand true love you will know that you should always choose to love people, even if you are not loved by them.

The cloud of living can never be pierced until a person knows and understands true love, for each and every idea and belief that can be convincingly argued for and that can pass all manner of human-made tests may fail only when tested against true love. Many are sincere when they declare their intentions to help their fellow human beings, yet if people should love each other they cannot really help anyone until they understand and give true love. It is difficult to describe the state of consciousness most of us live in for that consciousness argues against anything that might awaken us.

We see a distinct difference between those who truly understand love and those who either think they do or think they have discovered something more important than love. That distinction is clear only to those who truly know and understand love. Yet that which blinds those who think they understand love, but in fact do not, also makes it far, far more difficult for them to see any need to question their beliefs, let alone to search their heart, mind, and soul for that which they believe they have already found. Most people will never recognize that their lives and beliefs may need exploring and changing. The great danger to humanity is not any possibility that those who seek an understanding of love will not find it, but rather that most people will never complete their search.

Those who do not understand love often do not understand the need to understand love. The horror is that masses of people will live their lives following invisible patterns without ever allowing themselves to question their reason for living and will die without ever having sought an understanding of love. The solution? There is only one, and that is for you to search your heart, mind, soul, your very being, and know and understand love.

At the start of our discussion we asked you to put aside your questions about love until you completed your search, and knew and understood love. The answers to those questions, and the millions of other questions you will face throughout your life, can come only from your understanding of the love you found in your heart, mind, and soul. We have yet to find a single question that does not have real, true, pure, love as part of the answer. Those whose experience with "love" has been bad, those whose response to hate has been anger, those for whom love is simply one of several human emotions, none have understood and given the true love that is inside them.

If you have completed your search of heart, mind, and soul you already know the answer to the most difficult of questions. You know that choosing to love people is part of the answer to every question. Whether you realize it or not, you also know the rest of the answer, which we will discuss next.

Forever

If you understand love you know that if anything in life is worth living for it is for people to love, really and truly love, people. Yet if death is the end what use is it to love anyone? We believe that if death is indeed the end of your existence then love and hate and you and I and life are all transient puffs of smoke in an ultimately inanimate eternity. Even love will succumb to death making its apparent beauty no more lasting than a winter's snow.

We really do not know, and will not know, what lies in store for us beyond the grave until the inevitable moment of death arrives. If life and love end at the grave we will never know the answer for we will no longer exist and the question will die with us. Of course, such an end would take with it all the sad and glad and in between experiences of your lifetime. If you no longer are, you no longer are, period. The void that follows death without a life after death is a complete and total void. There would be no one to experience joy, there would be no one to experience pain, all would be as if it never was.

The possibility of nothing absolutely frees us to embrace the alternatives and to live our lives for the possibility that there is a non-physical life after physical death, or that physical life has existential meaning. If you do not agree that the possibility of meaning in our lives, and the freedom of nothing if we are wrong, is all that is required for us to live the most positive life we can, then you need to reread the chapters "Who Will You Be When You No Longer Are?", "You Can't Think About Nothing", and "Afraid of Nothing" until you understand what it means to say that there may be nothing after physical life.

We said there is absolutely no way we can prove life continues beyond the grave, but we also said there is absolutely no way we can prove it does not. We discussed the possibility of life having meaning without life after death. We said that we cannot be certain that life does not have meaning and purpose even if there is no life after death. While we cannot be certain we are right, we explained why we believe that life has meaning only if there is a non-physical life after death. We concluded that whether we are right or not, there is absolutely no reason not to live for the possibility that life has meaning and purpose, and for the possibility that we may eventually find true meaning and value in our life.

What connection does life on earth have with life after death? What does love on earth have to do with life after death? What can we say about the nature of life after death? We have once again returned to that murky area where intellect, insight, and intuition blend with belief and faith. We simply cannot know what life after death may or may not be like.

If there was nothing positive and good about life, the question of existence after death would be an academic one. Yet that seems not to be the case. We have said love is the very best one human being can give another human being. We have said that love is the most positive of human experiences. It is the deepest, most profound, of human relationships. It is the giving of all you have to give to someone else. If the most positive aspect of life is love, then a life after death that is filled with love seems to be worth believing in. If we continue to exist after death we may indeed find ourselves in a world where people love people.

If it is possible that we continue to exist after death, then should we not live for the possibility that life and love will continue after death? Those who complete their search and understand love understand that if love does not end at death then love is worth living for in this life and the next. It seems logically and intuitively clear that since you may continue to exist after death you should live with the hope that love has meaning and is worth living for in this life and that after physical death you will live forever in a world filled with never ending love.

If the only realistic alternative is nihilistic death, then it seems that you and everyone else should love each other and live for the possibility that we will continue to exist after death in an existence filled with love. Yet choosing love because the alternative is a meaningless death is not a good enough reason. Love must be chosen by those who in their heart, mind, and soul truly want to love, or their choice will be a shallow one that will not last. Those who choose to love must do so because they want to love.

Can we have faith in a random existence after death that has no guidance, might there be more? If we are to accept that human beings may continue to exist after the death of their bodies we need to consider what, if any, external force or presence may guide or control such existence. We are way past the limits of human comprehension, at the point where belief must turn into faith. The more modern science has discovered, the more it seems that some form of logical, rational, process occurs in nature, replacing random events with planned sequences.

Such logical progression of nature may be the result of an incredible computer like property whereby nature is equipped with some sort of artificial intelligence, perhaps so, perhaps not. Yet we have already said that the odds that our low entropy universe populated by sentient beings was created at random appear to be as close to zero as can possibly be imagined. Perhaps the universe is not controlled or guided by some deterministic process. Perhaps the universe is controlled or guided by someone. [Please read the next section in its entirety before reaching conclusions about what it says.]

God

Throughout human history there has existed in the majority of people a belief in some power, existence, a logical presence beyond human existence, a God (or gods). During at least the past few thousand years there has appeared in many cultures a belief in a God who is good, a God who wants human beings to do that which is good. Those who have completed their search of their heart, mind, and soul, know and understand love. Those who have completed their search know and understand in their heart, mind, and soul that it is good for people to love each other. Many believe that a God exists who gave us the love that is in our heart, mind, and souls. Many believe that a God exists who wants people to do that which is good, to love each other.

This belief in a God who wants people to love each other has its roots in intuitive feelings of humankind and in messages of prophets; and for those who believe in the divinity of Jesus, in the word of God himself. There will always be arguments that the messages are messages made up by the messengers, yet from all that we have discussed, from all that those who have completed their search know and understand about love, it seems that if God does exist the message from him would be for us to love one another, what many tell us it is.

We believe there is in most of us a feeling that God does exist. That feeling may be insight or it may be the result of a collective deep seeded desperation in human beings to be more than doomed animals. We will not know until our death, the definitive answer forever prohibited us by the limits imposed by our being no more than a part of that which we seek to explore. We are left at the point where faith must take over if we are to believe in the existence of God.

Perhaps the logical selections that appear to take place in nature cannot be explained by physical processes but rather represent actions taken by some indescribable presence, God, perhaps not. If our intuitive feelings and the scientific calculations that support them are correct, then the complex low entropy universe in which we live cannot be the result of random chance. If we are honest with ourselves, the only reasonable answer we can construct from objective observations based on current scientific knowledge as to why the low entropy universe in which we live exists is that it was designed and created to be as it is. If a Creator does not exist then the logical conclusion is that the universe in which we live would not exist and we would not be here.

Some people who believe that God does not exist believe that human beings can love and do good in a purely physical universe where there is no God. Is it possible that they are right? If human beings want to do good can they really do that which is good and meaningful if God does not exist?

If there is existential meaning to physical life that we do not or cannot understand, then perhaps even if God does not exist love may have meaning. We can never be certain that life does not have existential meaning. We cannot prove that if God does not exist and there is no life after death then living our lives, and doing that which is good, has no meaning. Because of the limitations of being only human we simply cannot rule out any possibility.

We said that, even though we cannot prove anything and may in fact be wrong, we believe that if we do not have a non-physical consciousness that continues to exist after physical death, then those who believe in nihilism are correct and some type of "nihilistic" void awaits all of us. It may be a true void, like the void that preceded our birth, or it may be a very strange void where billions of copies of us merely co-exist in a relativistic block universe. Whatever physical form it might take, it would seem to be a "meaningless" void. All would be as if it never was.

If physical death does annihilate our physical past, present, and future, then our life has meaning and purpose and value only if after our physical death our consciousness continues to exist in a non-physical life. We cannot prove that we continue, or do not continue, to exist after our physical death. Yet if there is a life after death, then it is reasonable to conclude that you will continue to experience a non-physical existence after your physical death, and that your life does in fact have meaning and value.

Is it possible that even if God does not exist there may be a non-physical existence after death which gives meaning and value to our life? The intuitive answer seems to be no. We cannot imagine a human spirit that survives death if there is no presence beyond life other than human spirits, if there is no Spirit greater than the human soul. It seems

134

intuitively unlikely that the only non-physical presence in the universe could be the human soul.

If there is no non-physical Spirit greater than the human soul, if there is no God, it makes no sense to conclude that a physical being born into our physical world has at birth, or somehow develops, a non-physical soul. We can see no possible way that a physical human being, who is a tiny part of an unimaginably huge universe, can survive physical death if there is no Spirit, no God, to grant that physical being, in some manner and fashion beyond our understanding, a non-physical soul and life. It somehow seems logically and intuitively true that without God there would be no reason to believe that we possess a consciousness that continues to exist beyond the death of our bodies, no reason to have hope that after our death we may live forever in a non-physical world. Even though it cannot be proven, it seems intuitively clear that if there is no Spirit greater than the human spirit, if God does not exist, then then there is no human soul and we do in fact cease to exist on our death.

Should we believe that God exists? If we were presented with the question of believing or not believing in the existence of a god of war or destruction, then it would not matter to us if he existed or not because his existence would give us no hope that love has meaning and is good. There would be no hope for an existence after our physical death in a heaven filled with love. We would choose not to believe in the existence of such a god.

However, the message of many about God, the message we accept, was and is that God wants every human being to do that which is good. The message that we choose to believe is true is that if God exists God wants every human being to love every other human being. We choose to have absolute faith that if God exists, God is good.

Saying that if God exists, God is good, does not prove that God exists, it does not even say that God exists. It says that if God exists, God is good, period. It says that if God exists, God is good, and that he wants each and every person to do that which is good. Even if you do not believe that God exists, or you are not sure what the "good" is that God would have us do in this world, in your heart, mind, and soul you know and understand that if God, the Creator of love, exists, God is good.

If you do not want evil to have power over good, if you do not want evil to fill the world instead of good, we cannot imagine why you would not choose to have absolute faith that if the presence greater than all else in this universe, the Supreme Being, God, exists, God is good. Whether you believe that God exists or that God does not exist, if you do not want to reject good and embrace evil, if you are not against good and for evil, there is no reason not to have absolute faith that if in fact God does exist, God is good.

It seems intuitively clear that if God, the One who is good, does not exist then there is no "heaven" where there is a life after death that is good. It is intuitively impossible for us to imagine the existence of a good life after death in a heaven filled with love where there is no Spirit greater than the human soul, where a God who is good is not present. We cannot imagine a heaven filled with perfect love that is created or sustained by imperfect human souls who during their physical lives repeatedly fail to choose love.

We cannot imagine a heaven filled with real, true, pure, love without the presence in heaven of One who loves with perfect love, without the presence of One who is good. It would seem that only God, the One who is good, could forgive human sins and cleanse human souls so that heaven would be filled with love. Without the presence of God who loves with perfect love, we cannot envision a heaven where human beings share real, true, pure, love. We cannot prove anything to be true, yet it seems intuitively clear that if God does not exist, there is no heaven.

We simply do not believe that there is a life after death in a heaven filled with love if God, the One who is good, the One who loves with perfect love, does not exist. We may be wrong, life may have existential meaning, yet it seems logically and intuitively true to us that without God each of us ceases to exist on the day of our death, annihilating our past, present, and future. It seems logically and intuitively true that without God, good and love and life are empty ideas that live and die with each human being.

We may believe that God exists, yet rather than belief, is the existence of God something we should have faith in? As we have said, having faith something is true is far more than believing it is true. We can say that those who have faith accept as true what they choose to believe is true, at least until proven beyond doubt to be untrue. Yet if you realize what it means to say that nothing can be totally proved or disproved, then what you choose to have faith in is in fact what you choose to accept as true for the rest of your life.

What you have faith in is not simply what you believe to be true, but rather what you choose to believe is true because in your heart, mind, and soul you want it to be true. You decide what you will have faith in, what you want to be true if anything at all is true. Having faith that something is true does not make it true, if it is not true it is not true. Yet if what you have faith in is in fact true it is true, period.

No matter how logical, rational, or scientific the arguments that are presented to you appear to be, we cannot prove that God exists or prove that God does not exist. We cannot prove that there is a life after death in a heaven or prove that a nihilistic death awaits us. Why then should you have faith God exists?

Again, if the message we conveyed to you about God was that he wants wars or sacrifices or other manner of destruction, then there would be no reason to have faith in him. But the message was and is that God who gave us love wants every human being to do that which is good. The message was and is that God wants every human being to love every other human being.

In our heart, mind, and soul we know and understand love. In our heart, mind, and soul we know and understand that it is good for each of us to love each other. If you have not completed your search of your heart, mind, and soul, if you do not yet understand that it is good to love each other, if you do not yet understand that we can and should do that which is good, then you will find it very difficult to find a reason to have faith in the existence of God. But if you have searched your heart, mind, soul, your very being, and know and understand love, you should want to, and choose to, have faith that a God exists who wants all people to do that which is good, a God who wants all people to love each other. If God does not exist then he does not exist, if God does exist then he does exist, period.

We believe that if God exists and gives each of us a non-physical life after death in a heaven filled with love, then our life both before and after physical death has meaning and value. We believe that if God exists, and in some manner beyond human comprehension grants existence to human beings even after the death of our bodies, then and only then life becomes more than a brief isolated event. Then, and only then, life and love have meaning and purpose and we can do that which is good.

Perhaps God has revealed to all or some of us that he exists. Yet even if God has not revealed this to you, he has given you the choice to have faith or not to have faith that he exists. Why should you have faith that God exists? Should we have faith that God exists because if God exists, God is good? We believe the answer to that question is that if we want good to exist and have meaning, if we want to do that which is good, we will choose to have faith that the Supreme Being, God, exists.

If love among people is good and meaningful and has purpose, it is good and meaningful and has purpose only if God exists and only because of God. If God makes it good for us to love each other in this life and in a world after death, and thus makes life worth living, then his existence alone gives us hope. It should be clear to all who want to do that which is good, who want to love, that they should have faith that God, the One who is good, exists.

It is God's will that we love each other, should we also love God? The answer to that question seems clear to us. We believe that without God, love would be destroyed by physical death and life would have no meaning or purpose. If our conclusions are right, without God there would be no reason for living. It is right to have faith in God and to love God, the One who is good. It is right to have faith in God and to love God, for without him love would be no more than one of many emotions that die with those who embrace them.

You should love God with the greatest love you can give. You should love God with all your heart, all your mind, all your soul, all your strength, for God alone makes it meaningful and right and good for us to love him and to love each other. You should love God with all your heart, all your mind, all your soul, all your strength, for God alone gives us hope that if we love him and love each other we will live forever in a joyous communion of love.

If you love God with all your heart, all your mind, all your soul, all your strength, you have chosen to do that which you can do, you can do no more, you should do no less. If you love God with all your heart, all your mind, all your soul, all your strength, you will do what God wants you to do, you will do God's will, you will love your neighbor as yourself.

Some two thousand years ago a man named Jesus said to all who would listen that God gave these commandments to all people, "You shall love the Lord your God with all your heart, and with all your soul, and with all your mind, and with all your strength." "You shall love your neighbor as yourself. There is no other commandment greater than these."

When asked who is my "neighbor" Jesus replied, "A man was on his way from Jerusalem down to Jericho when he fell into the hands of robbers, who stripped him, beat him, and went away leaving him half dead. It so happened that a priest was going down by the same road; but when he saw him, he went past on the other side. So too a Levite came to the place, and when he saw him he went past on the other side. But a Samaritan who was making the journey came upon him, and when he saw him he took pity on him. He went to him and bandaged his wounds, bathing them with oil and wine. Then he lifted him on his own animal, brought him to an inn, and took care of him there. The next day he took out two silver pieces and gave them to the innkeeper, and said, take care of him; and if you spend any more, I will repay you on my way back. Which of these three do you think was neighbor to the man who fell into the hands of the robbers?" The questioner answered, "the one who showed him kindness." Jesus said, "go and do likewise."

Who is your neighbor? With the possible exception of those who have totally rejected God, who if there is an eternal sin have committed the eternal sin (we briefly discuss the eternal sin in the Appendix), every person who loves you, every person who hates you, every enemy, every stranger, people of every continent, people of every race, every single human being in the entire world, everyone, is your neighbor. Jesus said that all who "keep the commandments" will live forever, continuing to exist after physical death in a state of never-ending joy.

Who was, or is, Jesus? Many people differ in who they believe Jesus to be. Many believe Jesus is the Son of God. There are many, many different beliefs as to what it means to say Jesus is God's son. Many believe Jesus was God incarnate. Other people believe Jesus was a prophet, given knowledge by God of the nature and meaning of life. Still others believe Jesus was not God but was a wise man with great insight into human existence.

Many people believe that Jesus and God are One, and that you must accept Jesus as God before you can know God and love God. We believe that even if you have not decided who you believe Jesus is, even if you do not believe that Jesus and God are One, you can and should love God with all your heart, with all your soul, with all your mind, with all your strength, and love your neighbor as yourself, and that out

139

of that love you will choose to believe, and have faith in, what your heart, mind, and soul leads you to believe or have faith about Jesus.

Whoever you have faith or believe Jesus to be or have been, his message about life remains the same: "On these two commandments hang all the law and the prophets", "You shall love the Lord your God with all your heart, and with all your soul, and with all your mind, and with all your strength", "You shall love your neighbor as yourself", "There is no other commandment greater than these", "do this, and you will live." If we love as God would have us love we are doing the very best that we can do. There is nothing else that we can and should do. It is your choice to love as God would have you love, or not, period.

When you complete your search it will be clear to you what God means when he tells you that you can and should love the Lord your God with all your heart, with all your soul, with all your mind, with all your strength. When you complete your search you will also know and understand what God means when he tells you that you can and should love your neighbor "as yourself". You will know and understand that you can and should love your neighbor "as yourself", as if he or she was in your place, as if he or she was "you". You should give your neighbor the food that you would give yourself, the water that you would drink, the shelter that you would provide for yourself, the clothing that you would wear, etc., even if you do not have enough left for yourself.

You should do to your neighbor what you would have them do to you. You should give your neighbor the food, water, shelter, and clothing that you would have them give to you. You should care for them when they are sick as you would have them care for you if you were sick. You should visit them when they are in prison as you would have them visit you if you were in prison. You should give your neighbor real, true, pure, love. You should love your neighbor "as yourself".

What about traditional religious beliefs, theology and doctrine, baptism, sainthood, communion, all the beliefs and observances generations have cherished. What role do they play in our discussion of love? If you understand love, the answer is clear that if you love God and your neighbor you will in every instance do the best you can to do what is right and good. That is all you can do.

Certainly loving God means you will help your neighbors when they are in need of help. Perhaps you will decide loving God requires you to make many changes in your religious beliefs, perhaps not. When you choose to love God and your neighbor every choice you make will be made out of love. It is the choice to love God as he would have you love him, and out of that love to love people as he would have you love them, that is the one important choice, all other choices will be governed by that one profound decision. To love God and our neighbor as God would have us love is the complete answer to all our questions.

Even though many believe that God has already spoken to us and that we have not listened, why does God not speak directly to each and every one of us and tell us that he exists? Perhaps God has not revealed to us that he exists in a manner that no one could question and has instead caused the observable physical universe to appear to follow deterministic laws, because he does not want us to know with absolute certainty that he does exist. Perhaps if we knew for an absolute fact that God exists, we would not choose to do God's will because we choose to love God and our neighbors, rather we would choose to do God's will to avoid loveless punishment. Perhaps God has not revealed to us that he exists so that we may have the freewill choice to have faith that God exists, and the freewill choice to love God and our neighbors, or not.

Why does God give us a choice to love or not to love? Why would God not create all of us in such a way that we must love as God would have us love? Perhaps the answer is that if evil did not exist, then not only would human beings not have a choice to do that which is bad, they would not have a choice to do that which is good. Perhaps if during our life on earth we did not have the freewill choice to do that which is good or do that which is bad, then we simply could not choose to love. Perhaps there is good and evil in this world so that we may choose love, and out of that love do that which is good.

We have completed a full circle back to the question, what is the meaning and purpose of life, yet it has become the question, should we believe God exists and have faith in him and love him? We have said that the reason we should have faith in and love God is because if God exists, God is good, he gives meaning and purpose to life and love, and he wants us to love him and to love each other. A "why not" argument can be made that if God does not exist nihilists are probably right and death is the end, but since God might exist we should do what he would want us to do or we might end up tortured in some form of eternal loveless punishment. That logic sounds good, yet it leaves us with a feeling that those who love to avoid punishment don't really love at all. If we are to have faith in God, and love as he would have us love, we must choose to love him because we want to love as he would have us love, not because we want to avoid the consequences of not loving.

After you have searched your heart, mind, and soul and know and understand love, you must choose whether or not to believe that there is nothing in the world better than people loving other people. If you agree love is worth living for, and if love has meaning only if God exists, then you must choose whether or not to live for the one hope for human beings, that God exists. You should not have faith in God because you want to avoid a loveless, eternal punishment. You should have faith in God and love God because God is good. You should have faith in God and love God because you want to do that which is good, you want to love God and your neighbor.

What do I believe and have faith in? If we love as God would have us love, what do I have faith will happen to us after our physical death? I have absolute faith that if God exists God is good. I have absolute faith that if after physical death we exist in heaven or in a loveless eternal life, God gives us the freewill choice to do that which if we do we will live forever in heaven in the presence of God, the One who is good. Think about the real, true, pure, love you found when you searched your heart, mind, and soul, and you will know and understand what love in heaven would be like.

After one moment in heaven, we will know that every single moment of our existence, our entire being, will be filled with real, true, pure love, forever. All the illness, pain, and sorrow we experienced during our life on earth will vanish completely. In an instant, memories of even the worst that happened to us before our death will be overwhelmed by the love that surrounds us and will "disappear" forever. We will exist in the presence of real, true, pure, perfect love, forever. We will exist in the presence of God.

After many, many years of thought and discussion, I believe that there are many difficult questions which have answers that are unclear, uncertain, or unknown; that there are many thoughts and ideas that language cannot adequately express; that there is knowledge beyond human ability to know; that we cannot "prove" anything unless truth is revealed to us; etc. After completing my search of my heart, my mind, and my soul, I believe that we do not need to answer all the difficult questions, express in words all that we intuitively feel, know what we cannot know, "prove" what is beyond human ability to prove, etc.

I have faith that God exists and that it is God's will that I "love the Lord my God with all my heart, with all my soul, with all my mind, with all my strength" and "love my neighbor as myself". I have faith that if each moment of each day I love as God would have me love, when I die I will have done all I could do, all I should do, and I will live forever in a heaven filled with joyful love.

Love the Lord your God with all your heart, with all your soul, with all your mind, with all your strength.

Love your neighbor as yourself.

You will make your choice.

Appendix - A Fanatic Life or a Normal Life

[If you have already read this appendix in LifeNotes please read it again, it contains a few additional thoughts.]

What will our life be like if we love God and our neighbors as God would have us love? This is a very, very, difficult question. It is clear that if we love God and our neighbors we will give food to a starving child, water to a thirsty stranger, shelter to someone who is homeless and cold. This intuitive truth is strong and basic. Is it always good to give a drink of water to a thirsty neighbor? There may be situations where we must choose to give water to one of two neighbors based on which neighbor has a greater need for the water. There may be times when we are physically prevented from giving water to a thirsty neighbor, or when there may be other negative consequences of doing so. Yet it is clear that the basic, fundamental, statement "we should give water to a thirsty neighbor" is always true.

So where does all that we have said leave us? Does it leave us with pragmatic, situation ethics, where that which is "good" is determined by individual circumstances? It does not. Perhaps God will forgive us if we love God and our neighbor with a lesser love, yet that does not change the fact that you can and should "love the Lord your God with all your heart, with all your soul, with all your mind, with all your strength" and "love your neighbor as yourself", nothing more, nothing less, period.

If I love a neighbor who is hungry and thirsty what will I do? The answer is that I will give them food and water. No matter how hard we have tried to find another answer, if we love our neighbor and our neighbor is hungry and thirsty, we cannot imagine not giving them food and water. If you know and understand the love that God has given us, you know and understand that there is no other answer. This alone tells us that if we love our neighbor as God would have us love, we will not live a "normal life", we will live a "fanatic life".

So, what will we do if we live a fanatic life? If you love your neighbor as yourself, you will share God's word with them by word and deed so that each and every one knows and understands that they can and should choose to do that which is good, that they can and should choose to do God's will and live a joyous life forever in heaven. You will share your food with the hungry even if you are left with not enough to eat, give your only coat to someone who is cold, and find shelter for all the homeless people you meet.

Even though you may agree with what we have just said, you need to recognize that it is incredibly difficult to live a fanatic life. It is relatively easy to accept that living a normal life filled with love for our family and friends is far better than living a life filled with selfish physical and emotional pleasure. It is not as easy to accept that a normal life is not the life that we should live, that it is not the "good life". It is extremely difficult to accept that we should live a life filled with fanatic and total acceptance of that which God would have us do.

This brings us to a very difficult question, if you "love the Lord your God with all your heart, with all your soul, with all your mind, with all your strength" and "love your neighbor as yourself", and you live in a world where many people do not choose to do God's will, will you ever do that which you would not do in a world where every person does God's will?

God has given each and every one of us the choice of giving food to our hungry neighbor or not. God has given each and every one of us the choice of doing physical harm to our neighbor or not. No matter what anyone else may choose to do, each of us has the choice to give food to a hungry neighbor or not, and each of us has the choice to do physical harm to a neighbor or not. We strongly believe that God would never have a neighbor choose not to give food to a hungry neighbor. We strongly believe that God would never have a neighbor choose to do physical harm to another neighbor. We simply do not believe that it is ever God's will that any of us choose not to give food to our hungry neighbor, or that any of us choose to do physical harm to our neighbor.

If your neighbor has plenty to eat yet is thirsty, and your neighbor refuses to share their food it is not God's will that you say to your neighbor "share your food and then I will give water to you". It is God's will that you love your neighbor as yourself and give them a drink of water if they are thirsty. If your neighbor is doing physical harm to their neighbor it is not God's will that you say to your neighbor "do not do physical harm to your neighbor and then I will not do physical harm to you". It is God's will that you love your neighbor as yourself and not do physical harm to them.

If we can kill one neighbor and prevent them from killing two other neighbors, it is not God's will that two people be killed, it is not God's will that one person be killed. It is God's will that no one is killed. If we do physical harm to reduce the physical harm done by another person there is one more person in the world who is doing physical harm, not one less. We are unwilling to conclude that God would have any of us do physical harm to our neighbor when each and every one of us has the choice to do physical harm or not to do physical harm, to kill or not to kill.

It is God's will that each and every moment of our lives each and every one of us do God's will, nothing less, nothing more, period. Our hope is that if we live a fanatic life we will have done God's will on earth, and after our physical death we will live a joyous life in heaven, nothing could be better.

What if we are wrong about God wanting us to live a "fanatic life"? We understand that if we are wrong, the physical consequences of choosing to live a fanatic life may be horrendous. We live in a world where people choose to do evil. If we do not use minimal physical force to prevent physical harm there will almost certainly be people who inflict excruciating pain and almost unimaginable tortures on our neighbors. If we do nothing to physically stop them there will almost certainly be parents who savagely beat infants, mass murderers who kill innocent children, and brutal political leaders who commit genocide. If we do nothing to stop those who choose to do evil there will almost certainly be more wars, slavery, rape, and murder.

Most view life after death as a separate existence from life on earth, where those people who made physical life on earth as "good" as it can be will live a joyous life in heaven. The collective wisdom of generations of human beings who want to do that which is good is that God would have us live a normal life. The vast majority of people, almost every person in the world, believes that we should do the best that we can to maximize the positive physical aspects of our lives on earth while minimizing the negative. Perhaps the billions of people, including virtually every theologian and philosopher, who believe that we can and should love God and family and friends with a more complex love are right.

A "normal life" most would consider to be a "good life" is a life where each individual has strong spiritual beliefs and faith which they gladly share with other people. Such a normal life may include a strong family unit, a loving spouse and kids, and close relationships with relatives. The parents have jobs they enjoy that provide sufficient income for the family's comfort, and that give them plenty of time at home. Family members and extended family enjoy talking, playing games, helping with homework, working around the house, eating out, going to movies, etc. The adults and kids participate in sports and hobbies and take family vacations each year.

A "good" normal life includes volunteer work at hospitals, soup kitchens, homeless shelters, etc., and generous donations to charitable organizations. The family accepts protection provided by police, military, and other government agencies using social programs, diplomacy, and the minimum force necessary to prevent one person from doing physical harm to another person. People who live such a "normal life" have a pleasant, happy, positive attitude toward all their neighbors, including family, friends, and strangers. Almost every human being who wants to love God and their neighbor will choose to live a "normal life" that maximizes the positive physical aspects of their life on earth, without causing what they consider to be unacceptable negative consequences for themselves and their neighbors.

This is a normal life that most people would call a good life. Indeed, almost everyone believes that this is the life that God would have us live. It is a life that focuses primary love and attention on family, and secondary love and attention on friends, while at the same time providing what each individual considers to be a generous amount of love, care, and help to those outside what is commonly known as their extended family.

Is this kind of normal life the life God would have us live, or not? We return to the question, if I love a neighbor who is hungry and thirsty what will I do? The answer is that I will give my neighbor food and water. Our conclusion remains the same, we strongly believe that God would have us live a fanatic life. Yet we may be wrong.

Perhaps we are wrong about God wanting us to live a fanatic life, perhaps God wants you to live a normal life which minimizes the negative and maximizes the positive. Even though we do not believe we are wrong, perhaps we are wrong and there is existential meaning and value in living a normal life even if there is no life after death. Perhaps if we choose to live a fanatic life we will not be choosing to do that which is good.

The modern world is an increasingly secular world. From birth to death we are immersed in societies which surround us with technology, social media, online influencers, celebrities, peer groups, direct messaging, streaming tv series, video games, consumer goods, fashion trends, new age media, life coaches, etc. We are part of a competitive, often hostile, global community. The environment we inhabit is alien to the family oriented agrarian lifestyle of our ancestors, for many it offers a far more comfortable place to live filled with physical pleasures. We are as able to choose a fanatic life as previous generations were, yet for most people in the world the contrast between a fanatic life and a normal life seems exponentially greater.

Even though we strongly believe that each and every one of us can and should live a fanatic life, we intuitively believe that very, very, very, very, very few, almost no one, will choose to live such a life. Almost everyone, including theologians and philosophers, who chooses to love God and their neighbor will choose to love God and their neighbor with a "lesser love" than God would have them choose. Almost everyone who chooses to love God and their neighbor will choose to live what they consider to be a good normal life.

God gave you the love that is in your heart, mind, and soul. God loves you. God forgives you not because of the good deeds you do, but because he loves you. We believe that God will forgive you if you love God and your neighbor, even with a lesser love.

If you, like almost every single human being in the world including the author, are not willing to accept the physical consequences of living a fanatic life, then live a normal life like the normal life we describe in this appendix. If you are unwilling to live a fanatic life, love God with as much of your heart, your soul, your mind, and your strength as you are willing to love him with and love your neighbor as much as yourself as you are willing to love them, with the hope that God will forgive you.

Complete your search of your heart, mind, and soul, and know and understand the true, pure, real, love that God has given us. Complete your search of your heart, mind, and soul, and know and understand God's will, what God would have you do. You will decide what you will do. You will make your choice.

Appendix - Distress & Depression

We have received comments from readers who tell us that our ideas caused them to be distressed or depressed. If you are one of those readers you need to consider the following. As human beings become anxious they often lose their focus and objectivity, and misinterpret what they are reading. If you understand what we are saying, there is absolutely no reason to be depressed by our ideas.

Why not? First, our conclusions may be right, we may have a permanent non-physical consciousness which gives meaning to life. Second, we may be wrong, life may have permanent existential meaning and value without a life after death. Third, if there is nothing after physical death you are free to live a life filled with both pain and joy, knowing that when you die the pain will be as if it never was.

No matter which of the three is right, depression and suicide may destroy the possibility of finding the meaning and purpose which may in fact exist in each and every human being's life and the possibility of living a joyful life after physical death. We are a small part of the whole. Unless the answer is revealed to us by the whole we can never know during our physical lives what really happens when our physical life ends. Life may have physical or non-physical meaning and value right now that we do not, and perhaps cannot during our physical lives, recognize and understand.

Beyond the fact that we cannot be sure we are right, nothing we have said changes the fact that all human beings can choose to do that which is good and live as positive a life as they can with the belief/faith that life may have meaning and purpose. This fact is extremely difficult to accept if you are searching for meaning in your life, you do not believe that there is a life after death, and you are discouraged or depressed before you start reading.

If your mind is not receptive and clear, when you read our ideas they may touch raw nerves and you may stop understanding what we are saying. If you do not agree that the possibility of "nothing" absolutely eliminates suicide as an option then carefully reread the four chapters beginning with "Who Will You be When You No Longer Are?" and this section until you understand why our conclusion is true.

There is no reason at all to reject the possibility that each of us has some kind of permanent physical or non-physical consciousness. There is no reason at all to reject the possibility that each of our lives may have meaning and purpose. There is no reason whatsoever not to search for an alternative to nihilism, to search for a reason for living, to seek meaning and purpose in our lives. We believe there is no reason not to explore and choose to have faith, as we have faith, in a non-physical consciousness and life after physical death.

There is absolutely no reason whatsoever not to live for the possibility, however remote you may believe it to be, that you can make choices now that will lead you to a positive life that has meaning and value. It is very important to understand that every person can live a positive life for the rest of their lives, loving their neighbor, doing that which is good, with the hope that physical life does have existential meaning and purpose and/or that there is a life after death. There is no reason whatsoever to be depressed, there is every reason to do that which is good. If you believe suicide is an option seek professional help now!

Call 988 on your phone to reach the nationwide Suicide & Crisis Life-line.

Appendix - Eternal Sin

If we have the freewill choice to love God or not to love God, and the freewill choice to love our neighbor or not to love our neighbor, then it would seem that we have the freewill choice to reject God and love, or not. Those who choose to reject God, who are against God, who blaspheme God, appear to have chosen to separate themselves from God, forever. Jesus said that even though all else will be forgiven, there will be no forgiveness in this world or the next for those who blaspheme the Holy Spirit, they have committed the eternal sin.

Perhaps you have not completed your search and do not have faith in God. Perhaps you do not believe that God exists. No matter what you believe, if God does exist then God exists, period. No matter what you believe to be true, whether you believe that God exists or does not exist, if you do not want to choose evil over good, you must never blaspheme the Holy Spirit, you must never reject God, you must never be against the One alone who is good.

We have readers who indicate that they are distressed and depressed by the possibility that they may have committed the eternal sin. If God exists and if there is an eternal sin, then God gives us the choice to commit the eternal sin or not to commit the eternal sin. It would seem that those who have not committed the eternal sin would be distressed if they believed that they might have committed the eternal sin. It would seem that the very fact that someone is distressed by the belief that they may have committed the eternal sin may suggest that they have in fact not committed the eternal sin.

Physical and mental disorders cause extreme anxiety and depression and may lead a person to believe that they have committed the eternal sin when in fact they have not. If you are distressed and depressed by the possibility that you have committed the eternal sin you need to talk with religious counselors. Talk to several people, especially mental health professionals if there is any possibility at all of psychological or emotional influences or problems, so that you may better determine what you have and have not done.

It can be very difficult to find qualified professionals, and even when you do find them, it can be very difficult to tell them about your fears. Find qualified professionals and talk to them. You need to overcome any reluctance you may have to talk with those who might help and be willing to allow them to help you decide what you really believe is true.

Seek professional help now!

Call 988 on your phone to reach the nationwide Suicide & Crisis Lifeline.

.

Contact and Other Books

Our books, LifeNotes and LOVE - In Search of a Reason for Living, are available in FREE eBook editions on our website LifeNotes.org and in the Apple, Google, and Amazon bookstores ($1 from Kindle).

They are also available in paperback from Amazon and other bookstores.

If you would like to help us maintain our publications please send a contribution to:

LifeNotes, 838 E High St Box 130, Lexington, Ky 40502

email: comments@ws5.com

V-11-11-11.03-11-23-U